COOKBOOK of SHADOWS

simple recipes for
POWERFUL
MAGICK

About the Author

Melanie Marquis is an award-winning author of many books including *Llewellyn's Little Book of Moon Spells*, *Carl Llewellyn Weschcke: Pioneer and Publisher of Body, Mind, and Spirit* (IPPY Gold Medal winner for Best Biography), *Beltane*, *Lughnasadh*, and *A Witch's World of Magick*. She is also the creator of *The Modern Spellcaster's Tarot* (illustrated by Scott Murphy) and *The Stuffed Animal Tarot* (with Aidan Harris and Mia Harris). She is the producer of Mystical Minds Convention and other local, regional, and national events. She is also the creator of @ StuffedAnimalMagickShop channel on Tiktok and You-Tube. Book a tarot reading or purchase magickal housewares, spice blends, and folk art at MelanieMarquis.com

MELANIE MARQUIS

COOKBOOK
of SHADOWS

simple recipes for
POWERFUL
MAGICK

Llewellyn Publications | Woodbury, Minnesota

FIRST EDITION
First Printing, 2024

Author photo by Andrew Harris
Book design by R. Brasington
Cover design by Shira Atakpu
Editing by Laura Kurtz
Interior art by Llewellyn Art Department

Llewellyn Publications is a registered trademark of Llewellyn Worldwide Ltd.

Library of Congress Cataloging-in-Publication Data (Pending)
ISBN: 978-0-7387-7496-1

Llewellyn Worldwide Ltd. does not participate in, endorse, or have any authority or responsibility concerning private business transactions between our authors and the public.

All mail addressed to the author is forwarded but the publisher cannot, unless specifically instructed by the author, give out an address or phone number.

Any internet references contained in this work are current at publication time, but the publisher cannot guarantee that a specific location will continue to be maintained. Please refer to the publisher's website for links to authors' websites and other sources.

Llewellyn Publications
A Division of Llewellyn Worldwide Ltd.
2143 Wooddale Drive
Woodbury, MN 55125-2989
www.llewellyn.com

Printed in the United States of America

Other Books by
Melanie Marquis

Llewellyn's Little Book of Moon Spells (2020)

Modern Spellcaster's Tarot (2016)

A Witch's World of Magick (2014)

Carl Llewellyn Weschcke: Pioneer and Publisher of Body, Mind, and Spirit (2018)

Contents

Section 5: Recipes for Magickal Goals 101

Section 6: Cooking with the Seasons 169

Section 7: Ingredients 215

Recipes

Preface

Thanks to my creative, psychic, and "spiritual but not religious" mother, I grew up believing in magick and seeing it as a commonplace part of daily life just like cooking dinner every evening. In fact, the two were often intertwined. I remember watching my mom sprinkle cinnamon, sugar, and unknown other spices on ordinary toast that was about to become extraordinary. "Let me sprinkle on some love," she'd say with a twinkle in her eye, her little fingers making circular motions over the bread. "And let me put in the monkey–Ook! Ook!" she'd say with sincerity. Sometimes, she let *me* put in the monkey. This was how we made what she called "Monkey Bread," basically a variation of cinnamon toast but with a name she knew I could not resist. Her recipe proved to be so successful that she soon added more variations of "Monkey Bread" to our meal and snack rotations. Old bread with gravy? Monkey Bread! Pizza made with cheese slices and spaghetti sauce on hot dog buns because there isn't any actual pizza, or regular bread? Monkey Bread! Whatever the Monkey Bread variation my mom was serving up, I was always happy and eager to enjoy it. My mom grew up in the southern U.S., and she knew how to make food taste good. The meals she cooked were never gourmet or complex, but they were always tasty and made you feel special.

My dad was also a wizard in the kitchen, or at least, I perceived him as such. He didn't believe in magick per se but could still make fantastical things happen when it came to food. He had the timing for frying corn tortillas down to the second and the mystical ability to turn stale bread and burnt toast into flavorful croutons. He always let me help him grate the cheese on taco night, which was often multiple times a week in our southern Arizona household where we lived within walking distance from the U.S.-Mexico border. My dad loved to explain how clever and more economical it was to grate your own cheese rather than buy it pre-shredded or pay extra to have the deli clerk shred it. This train of thought would inevitably lead him into talking about the virtues of croutons, and how a person could save a lot of money making their own. In my seven-year-old eyes, he was an absolute genius, and I tried to convince him that we should make our own crouton factory. He wasn't a great cook, but he wasn't a bad one, either. He really only cooked tacos, croutons, and maybe the occasional scrambled eggs with ketchup or Tabasco sauce, along with grilled cheese sandwiches with tomato soup. However, he still managed to convey to me the great value and importance that food held in our lives. He never let us waste any scraps when cutting vegetables. He would peel and cut onions with such precision that no usable bits were ever wasted.

He had the ability, like I do and his mother had, to make soup out of virtually anything and practically nothing.

My grandma was so extreme in her cooking frugality that she truly could have accidentally poisoned somebody. I guess my dad naturally picked up some of her waste-adverse ways. One time, she served us a meal and then told us that the green beans and meat we just ate had been in her possession for well over a decade. The food had moved with her from her home at the Grand Canyon where she had raised my dad and his twin brother, to her next home in northern Arizona, to her current home in southern Arizona. She didn't perceive this as being strange at all, having grown up dirt poor and being grateful for the soup her mother had made from actual garbage scraps her dad would salvage through his sporadic work as a trash collector.

My dad didn't see anything wrong with fourteen-year-old food, either. He never understood why my mom always managed to make up an excuse for why we couldn't accept grandma's dinner invites. After this particular incident, my mother discreetly informed me and my siblings that we were not to eat foods that came from grandma's freezer or canning jars. In fact, with the exception of toast, crackers, and peanut butter, there was only one other thing we were allowed to consume at grandma's house: the "Sun Tea" that always seemed to be brewing on her doorstep and was said to contain "Arizona sunshine" as a main ingredient.

At any rate, all these influences taught me early on that cooking could create miracles. It could make fourteen-year-old food edible. It could turn stale cornbread into delicious stuffing, it could transform the tiniest vegetable scraps into savory soups to feed a whole family.

I wanted to learn this magick myself: the magick to make anything taste good, the magick to make something out of nothing, the magick to make simple ingredients into something special and use the intrinsic power and beauty of each ingredient to the fullest. As I've learned about the magickal properties of plants, herbs, and spices throughout my many years of witchcraft practice, this knowledge has naturally melded into my cooking practices, empowering me to make the most of my meals and really appreciate the power, magick, and nourishment each ingredient brings.

For many people, maintaining a healthy relationship with food is a struggle. Including magick in the cooking process that can help cultivate positive associations and connections to food that can inspire us to make cooking and eating choices that nourish and support us, physically and spiritually. There are many aspects and layers to cooking magick and ways to activate the potential of food to nourish not just your body but your mind and spirit as well. From the choice of dishes to make, to the selection of ingredients, to the cooking techniques, every step in the cooking process can be infused with magick.

This book is your guide to exploring just how easy and rewarding cooking can be, and what a versatile and natural medium for magick it is. Most of the recipes call for simple ingredients you might already have in your pantry, and many of the recipes invite adaptation and customization. Cooking doesn't have to be complicated in order to produce tasty results, and magick doesn't have to be complex in order to be effective. Whether you're brand new to cooking or an experienced chef, let this book of simple recipes for powerful magick inspire your creativity and boost your confidence in both the culinary and magickal arts.

Acknowledgments

Thank you to my son Aidan and my daughter Mia for testing all the recipes in this book and for all the happy times we have cooking together and eating together. Thank you to my editor Elysia Gallo for your support and vision in helping this project come to life. And special thanks to Aldo Ludovico for your extraordinary motivation, inspiration, and encouragement as I saw this book through to completion, and for indulging my musings about whisks and magick.

Introduction

· ✦ ☆ ✦ ·

What is Magickal Cooking?

Magickal cooking is a cooking style that empowers us to shape reality through mindful food preparation techniques that enhance the metaphysical energies and natural qualities of ingredients. Knowing how to cook more mindfully and intentionally will help you benefit from the magick of food in new ways. This book is a cookbook, a spellbook, and a magickal reference designed to help you make more magick more often and more easily, while creating some delicious, easy-to-prepare meals in the process. The recipes are mostly simple so that it's easier to focus on the magick at hand, as well as to minimize the frustration of having to acquire an abundance of hard-to-find and costly ingredients just to try a new recipe. Beginning cooks will build foundational cooking skills, while more experienced cooks will find room for customization. This book is designed to become your own personalized Cookbook of Shadows, with built-in spaces for you to add your own magickal correspondences and other notes about ingredients.

Cooking is naturally magickal, important to humankind in truly existential ways. Not only does it make a lot of foods much more enjoyable to eat, it also makes more foods safer to eat. Cooking can kill bacteria and parasites, making certain foods edible that would otherwise be potentially dangerous. It allows us to transform bland or bitter ingredients into tasty morsels. It gives us the ability to feed an entire family by combining a multitude of food scraps not large enough for one.

It provides us a medium for creativity and expression—cooking truly is an art as well as a craft. Cooking is a necessary part of daily living that gives us an opportunity to honor ourselves and our loved ones through the foods we are preparing, serving, and consuming.

Through the magick of cooking, the meals we create can connect us, soothe us, energize, and protect us. A good meal can transform a mood just as it can a moment. It's an ancient wisdom that guides us to cook with love, and magickal cooking is no different: Let your heart guide your magick, and let your love pour into the food you make to be received by all who eat it. This book is a resource for you to use for information and inspiration to cook your own meals made from the heart.

How to Use This Book

This book is designed to be versatile and user friendly. At the beginning, you'll find essential information about the techniques you can use to add magick to your cooking and unlock the full power of food. Next, you'll find foods and recipes aligned with the elements and an explanation of how you can use these elemental alignments as a reliable framework for crafting your own cooking magick. There's also a section outlining the celestial alignments of common foods, including recipes created to correspond with the sun, moon, and the planets in our solar system. After that, you'll find ingredients and recipes organized by the magickal goal or effect you might be going for, whether it's psychic power, protection, peace, prosperity, love, strength, joy, courage, calm, purification, health, or success. Finally, you'll find information on common ingredients including their magickal qualities and how to prepare them, as well as a sampling of mystical lore and superstitions surrounding them picked up from my own experiences and traditions. You'll find here also extra lines for you to add your own beliefs and food customs.

The recipes are simple, versatile, easy to prepare, and generally inexpensive, making it easy to customize and fun to experiment. If you're an experienced cook and Kitchen Witch, this book can serve as a handy reference for ingredient correspondences and recipe ideas. If you're fairly new to cooking or magick, you'll find your mystical and culinary skills and confidence growing rapidly as you learn to prepare simple, wholesome ingredients in a way that maximizes the magickal potential of food.

Section 1

* ✦ ⛤ ✦ *

The Basics

The recipes in this book are designed for magickal effect based on the ingredients they include, but they're also designed to be tasty. Flavor comes first in cooking magick! In some instances, you might find yourself wanting to add an ingredient to a recipe for its magickal effect rather than for its flavor. It's helpful to know you can use tiny quantities of an ingredient to impart magickal power to a recipe without affecting the overall taste. Likewise, it's also okay to use ingredients that don't necessarily go with the magickal flow of your recipe. Just ahead in this book, you'll learn how to supercharge ingredients so that your dish shines in the ways you want it to shine.

Another major point to remember is that food cooked with love tastes better! Think of your feelings for the people you are cooking for as you prepare the food. The power of your emotions will ultimately transfer to the eaters. Food cooked with feeling maximizes the power of your ingredients, and any magickal effects will be more pronounced.

While putting feeling into your food is important, so too is knowing the ingredients you're using. When utilizing ingredients that are new to you, first be sure to feel it, smell it, and taste it when possible before adding it to your recipe. Doing so helps you understand the ingredient's energies, strength, and flavor profile.

There are a myriad of ways to make magick in the kitchen. This book will show you different ways to impart magick to food through choice of ingredients as well as techniques that transform basic food preparation maneuvers into powerfully magickal actions.

Cooking magick requires respect and understanding of the fact that food is absolutely essential to every single one of us. Our survival, success, well-being, and happiness literally depend on it. It's important to show gratitude for the magick and blessings of food in order to cultivate a closer relationship to the earth and its various bounties. Doing so increases the power of your magick exponentially.

One way to honor your food and express gratitude for its blessing is to always cook with care. This means being appreciative of even the humblest ingredients. Nearly every food can be made to taste good if you know how to prepare it properly. Cooking with care also means taking steps to not ruin food through improper cooking or lack of attention, nor waste food by cooking too much and not properly preserving and utilizing leftovers. Save the scraps when prepping vegetables, and cook them all

together in water with a lot of savory spices to create your own homemade vegetable broth. You can include oregano, garlic, parsley, pepper, celery, carrots, onions, tomato, or any other flavorful veggie scraps you have on hand. To create a soup from your broth, just add any vegetable, meat, or noodles. You can even add tortilla strips or homemade croutons to bulk it up.

Another way to show gratitude for food through minimizing waste is to plan your leftovers. For example, if you have black beans one night, you can turn it into chili the next night, then mix the chili with rice to use on burritos another night.

You can also create compost from organic kitchen waste and use it to help you grow your own herbs and vegetables. Cooking food you grew yourself is its own kind of magick that brings additional power to your meal. There's also no better way to learn about an ingredient than to grow it yourself, prepare it, and eat it. Many herbs can be grown in small containers right in your kitchen.

Also keep in mind these kitchen safety basics:

- Keep a fire extinguisher in the kitchen, and be sure to have a working smoke alarm. While you shouldn't expect to start any fires while cooking, equipment malfunctions, electrical fires, grease fires, and other mishaps and mistakes can and do happen to anybody.
- Consider installing a fire guard behind the stove to help reduce the chances of a kitchen fire spreading.
- If you must leave the stove while something is cooking, utilize a kitchen timer or set an alarm on your phone to alert you when food needs attention.
- Never leave hot oil unattended, not even for a couple of minutes! Be sure you're ready to be at the stove until the frying is complete before you start heating the oil.
- Never mix water and hot oil! Water mixed with hot oil will violently pop and splatter, causing risk of injury and fire. Keep your hands dry while frying foods. Also be sure any spatulas or other utensils you're using are completely dry before placing them in the hot oil.
- Be careful when adding foods to hot oils. Lean back slightly and stand straight so that your face is not hovering directly over the pan before gently lowering the food into the oil. If you drop

it from too high up, it can splash and get on the burner and catch on fire or get on your skin and cause a painful injury.

- When frying foods in hot oil, always have handy (in addition to the fire extinguisher kept in the kitchen) a lid for covering the pan and some salt for sprinkling on any small sparks.
- Take care where you place your potholder. Be sure it's never close enough to stovetop burners to catch fire.
- Beware of using a wet potholder! Water conducts heat, and a potholder will not be as effective if it has accidentally been placed in a kitchen spill.
- Some foods should never be left unattended. Those foods include fudge, candies made on the stovetop, custards, risottos, sugar syrups, deep fried foods, gravies, and basically anything cooking in hot oil, anything with sugar as its main ingredient, or anything cooking in the oven on broil.

Section 2

Techniques

There are many ways to enjoy the magick of cooking, and the techniques you choose to employ will shape and expand your experience. You might create a meal designed to be magickal on every level, or you might only employ a single technique or two into each meal you make.

Choosing and Using Ingredients

One way to transform meals into magick is to choose a recipe based on the magickal qualities of the ingredients. Every food has the ability to bring magick into your life. When you eat, you are consuming the energy that has brought the food to this point in time to be eaten by you. You are connecting with the energies of the foods you eat, and through those foods, you are connecting also with the energies that went into its growth. When you eat an orange, you are eating also the sunshine that helped it grow. You are consuming the energy of the microbes that fed the soil that sustained the tree that bore the orange. You are enjoying the fruits of Nature and the fruits of those who worked hard in Nature's cultivation. An orange you might eat was once a part of a unique living thing that may very well still exist. To eat an orange or any other food is to connect with a unique creation of Nature, a creation connected to different aspects of the universe just as you are. These connections allow you to draw in specific energies and structure circumstances more favorably.

Many of the magickal connections and correspondences of common foods and spices are outlined in these pages, but you should also feel confident utilizing your personal associations with different foods. For instance, if your very strong and protective grandfather always loved blueberries, this fruit will most likely be a good ingredient to add energies of strength and protection to your day.

It's also a good idea to trust your intuition if you feel strongly about a particular ingredient, even if it seems to go against traditional lore. Research your hunches. Be aware that there is a ton of misinformation floating around (especially online!) regarding magickal correspondences. It's a good idea to do your own research to learn the basis and reasoning for assigning various plants and herbs various correspondences. You might still disagree with the generally agreed upon view of a particular ingredient, but if your reasoning is sound, you can most likely trust in your estimation.

To get a feel for an ingredient's qualities, notice and appreciate its look, smell, and texture. Taste it if it's safe to eat uncooked. Try to describe the energies you sense in it, then look at other references to compare your impressions and see if anything you intuited is corroborated or contradicted. Where your impressions are contradicted, do further research to find out whether or not the contradictions have a reasonable basis, and experiment further with the ingredient to get to know more about it.

Keep in mind that there isn't a food on earth that has only one, single attribute. Just as humans are complex, all living things are complex. We all—plants and animals alike—have a plethora of qualities and characteristics that make us each a unique combination of similarities. Just as you can be kind in one moment and angry in another, so too can a food show different attributes at different times.

Notes on Substitutions

Most of the recipes here are designed to be customizable to suit your own dietary needs and preferences. For those on a gluten-free diet, most of the recipes that call for flour can be made with almond flour, hemp flour, oat flour, rice flour, or other gluten-free alternatives. If you're on a low- or no-sugar diet, try substituting agave nectar, honey, stevia, or unsweetened applesauce in recipes that call for white or brown sugar. In recipes where milk, cheese, eggs, butter, other dairy products, or meat is called for, plant-based alternatives can be utilized if desired. It's no secret that industrial large-scale dairy, meat, and egg production involves a lot of practices that cause the animals extreme discomfort and suffering. When cooking for magickal effect, it's best to have the energies of the recipe be as harmonious as possible. You might consider finding a trusted local source for animal products or looking for the most ethical options at the grocery store.

Supercharge Your Food

To supercharge your ingredients to be in harmony with the vibe and effect you want your meal to have, you'll need to do something to activate them. Feel the essence in the ingredient that you wish to be most pronounced, then think of this growing stronger and stronger. To save time, you can charge ingredients by placing them near crystals, stones, magickal symbols, or even tarot cards that correspond to your goal. For instance, the joy-bringing qualities of oranges could be activated by placing the orange on top of the Sun tarot card or by surrounding the fruit in a ring of citrine crystals. When it comes time to mix each ingredient into your recipe, visualize with feeling and clarity the specific effects you want the ingredient to produce, then think of those energies either dominating or enhancing the other ingredients in the dish.

Magickal Tools

Similarly to how an ingredient might be charged up and activated for maximum magick, so too can everyday kitchen utensils and cooking equipment be charmed to help you achieve different goals. Enchanting your tools beforehand saves time. For example, you might keep a special spoon charmed to bring peace or choose a favorite bowl to associate with love and friendship. To enchant and empower your kitchen tools, call on a higher power or spirit of your choosing and ask that entity to grace your tool with their power. Another way is to conjure up an abundance of the energy you wish to impart to the tool, and project that concentrated energy into the item. Envision the energy you're projecting literally meshing together with the energetic structure of the object. You might call on the energies of the sun, moon, earth, or elements to come into your kitchen tools and dwell there. You can charm your blender, knives, spatulas, whisks, garlic presses, graters, peelers, spoons, pots, pans, even the oven itself.

Magickal Maneuvers

Cooking often requires actions such as stirring, cutting, flipping, mashing, and draining, and you can easily transform these everyday cooking maneuvers into magickal actions.

Stirring

As you stir foods, think of the energies blending. Stir clockwise to draw things in and to visualize energies expanding and growing stronger. Stir counterclockwise to send things away and to cause energies to weaken. Trace an infinity symbol or stir in a spiral starting in the center and moving outward to magnify. Trace an "X" to banish, destroy, or diminish. Stir in a pentacle shape to bring money or protection, or stir in Jupiter's symbol to change your luck for the better. Stir in the shape of a heart to convey love, or scatter ingredients using a fork to cause energies to break apart and be undone.

Cutting

Cutting food is a powerful way to visualize cutting through obstacles or destroying something you wish to overcome. Imagine whatever it is you are wishing to get past being broken down into tinier, more manageable bits with each cut you make. Cutting can also be used to release the hidden power that dwells in food. Envision each slice of the knife unleashing the energy of the ingredient, slashing through its bonds to free it to do its thing in the recipe. You might decide to supercharge one knife with the power to destroy any obstacle, and supercharge another knife to magnify the power of the ingredients it slices.

Mashing and Grinding

Mashing, grinding, chopping, pureeing, or otherwise macerating ingredients is another way to release the power of the food. Like slicing food with a knife, any of these actions can also be used as a medium for magick to help destroy obstacles and negative forces more easily. Choose an ingredient to represent the obstacle, and mash it by hand using a mortar and pestle, or chop it into oblivion with a spin in the blender.

Flipping

If you're cooking something that will need to be flipped over at some point, you can utilize the action for magick much like a tarot card might be employed for spellwork. For example, if you've been in a rut, you might think of a piece of toast as that rut. Once the top toasts, think of the current rut being toasted away, and flip it over as you envision yourself enjoying the new experiences you desire.

Draining

The act of draining can be used similarly. For example, you might add a small amount of pepper to the water when cooking pasta to symbolize something you wish to be rid of, then imagine that draining away as you drain the noodles, replacing it with sauce and spices that symbolize the energies you wish to invite in your life in abundance.

Style It Your Way

While the recipes in this book are all designed to have a magickal effect based on ingredients and general method described in the recipe, incorporating these little extras of cooking magick can make a big impact. Challenge yourself to try these techniques of magickal cooking, and think of additional ways you can incorporate more magick into the common actions that are part of the process. Most of the recipes describe basic food preparation techniques and the general magickal attributes or effects of the recipe, but it's up to you to choose the specifics. What is your specific, personal goal for the magick you want the food to impart? Will you use any special stirring or slicing techniques? Will you add or subtract any ingredients to better reflect your particular magickal aim? As the cook and the magick maker, it's part of your craft to choose the attributes of ingredients you wish to highlight in any given recipe, and it's part of your art to bring magick to the process in a way that seems right to you for the moment.

Section 3

✦ ◆ ☆ ◆ ✦

Cooking with the Elements

Elemental magick is a method of understanding and working with the powers of Nature through a simple framework that makes it easy to design spells and magickal charms that work. Commonly but not universally used in witchcraft, the system of elemental magick describes Nature as being composed of four earthly elements: fire, water, earth, and air—plus a fifth element of spirit that unites all the others. Fire includes the sun, warmth, light, and lightning and is sometimes equated with the lifeforce, courage, strength, energy, passion, success, and illumination. Water includes the moon, oceans, rivers, ponds, lakes, streams, groundwater, rain, snow, sleet, and hail. The water element is associated with creativity, quenching thirsts, love, purification, and healing. It is considered to rule over the body's fluids, including blood. The element of air rules the skies and the atmosphere. It equates with the winds, the breath, thought, knowledge, movement, change, and transformation. The earth element encompasses mountains and rocks, Earth's crust and mantle, dirt and soil. This element equates with foundation, stability, strength, protection, prosperity, truth and sincerity, health and vitality, growth and abundance. The earth element rules flesh and bones.

This framework provides a convenient starting point for making magick. If you know your goal and the element that rules over that domain, you can petition the forces of Nature associated with that element for assistance in achieving your aims.

It's important to note that these elements are neither separated in Nature nor in magick: everything is interconnected and interdependent. As living creatures of the earth, we rely on all the different aspects of Nature working together in harmony.

Thinking about the earth and its magick in terms of the elements simply gives us humans a way of perceiving things that can make designing spells and learning to work with the powers of Nature a little easier. In cooking magick, utilizing a framework of elemental magick will make it easy for you to choose spices and ingredients that are just right for your goal.

You'll find that most ingredients have more than one association. This is because nothing in Nature is only one thing; every living thing has a multitude of attributes. In addition, herbalists are not always in agreement as to a particular plant's associations, nor are the most traditional and most accepted herbal correspondence guides. Confusion can also arise because different parts of a plant might be given different elemental associations. Carrots, for instance, are commonly associated with the earth element because they grow underground. The green leafy tops of carrots, however, are associated with the air element due to their delicate and lacy leaf structure. Just as scientists may have debated initially on how to characterize the duck-bill platypus, herbalists aren't always in consensus when it comes to categorizing plants. Some disagreement is inevitable, given the subjective nature of the process. In truth, all plants have the natures of all the elements within them, at least to a degree, as it takes all four elements to create every single plant on earth. Take oranges, for example. When you think of an orange's most defining characteristics, what comes to mind? It is round like the earth, and its color is like the fiery sun, yet it is juicy like water, and eating it is invigorating like a breath of fresh air. So which element does it correspond to? While the general consensus is fire, due to the fruit's association with the sun based on its shape, color, and energizing nature, an argument could also be made that it should be associated instead with water because it's so juicy and refreshing. This is to say that the process of assigning elemental attributes and other magickal correspondences to plants is not an exact science. Such designations are guided by both objective and subjective criteria based on a plant's color, structure, growth pattern, energetic "feel," taste (if edible), effects if medicinal, its botanical lineage, and any mythology or folklore surrounding it.

Every plant has its own standout, defining characteristics, and it is these more dominant aspects that guide the assignment of correspondences.

While most herbalists would agree that having a hot taste and a red color would align most closely with the fire element, not all herbalists would agree that a particular plant's hot taste and red color are its defining characteristics. The radish is a perfect example: a radish certainly has a hot, peppery taste and is red in color, but it's also cool, white, and watery on the inside—characteristics of the water element. What's more, it grows underground, an earth element characteristic. So where would *you* assign it? The system of elemental attributes is a tool to help you choose recipes or design your own based on your magickal needs or desires of the moment. The correspondences provided are based on the author's personal witchcraft practice, knowledge of herbs, culinary experience, and intuition, corroborated in most cases by traditional astrological herbalism and herb lore, and/or the work of more modern herbalists such as Scott Cunningham.

Fire

The element of fire represents the power of the sun and the sometimes controllable and useful, sometimes uncontrollable and destructive, nature of fire. The element of fire confers energy, courage, and strength. Including ingredients aligned with the fire element in your cooking helps clear away negative energies, increase protection, bring strength, and encourage passion. All hot and spicy foods are attuned with the fire element. As you add these ingredients to your recipes, think of the heat they bring to the food. Think of the essence of fire and envision these energies growing stronger as you prepare your food. If you're using the fire element for protection or purification to clear away and banish negative energies, think of the fire essence of the food driving out any negative energy or baneful presences, keeping away any threats. Think about its essence being so hot that it's intolerable to anything or anyone who stands against you. Envision the food nourishing your cells with a protective power that will drive out anything harmful. If you're using the fire element to invigorate a situation or increase courage, energy, strength, passion, or stamina, envision the fiery essence of your ingredients charging the rest of the food and your body with an energy of excitement. Think of fireworks, lightning. Imagine yourself or the people you wish to energize being ridiculously energized, doing backflips and jumping up and down. Visualize yourself picking up something that weighs a thousand pounds with great ease as you prepare your fire-aligned meal. Fire foods work well with Earth foods that bring greater strength and stamina and more lasting power.

Cooking Methods
Heating foods in any way, cooking over open flame, grilling, frying, sautéing, baking.

Ingredients
Fire-aligned foods include anything spicy, especially if the food is red or orange in color, and many foods closely associated with the sun:

Allspice

Any hot sauce

Black pepper

Chili powder

Chilies or peppers (jalapeños, poblanos, bell peppers, etc.)

Cinnamon

Corn

Cumin

Fennel

Garlic

Ginger

Horseradish

Mustard

Onions

Oranges

Paprika

Radishes

Red beans

Red kidney beans

Red pepper

Rosemary

Sunflower seeds

Wasabi

White pepper

General notes

_____

_____

_____

_____

_____

_____

_____

_____

_____

_____

EASY FIRE CHILI

Effects: Eat for strength, protection, and courage.
Makes: 8 to 10 servings

Ingredients

2 cans or 3½ C prepared dried dark red kidney beans

1 can or 1¾ C prepared dried black beans

1 can stewed or 1¾ C diced tomatoes

1 onion, diced

1 bell pepper, diced

½ tsp salt

1 tsp chili powder

¼ tsp cumin

¼ tsp black pepper

1 tsp garlic powder

1–2 tbsp hot sauce (optional)

2 small jalapeños, diced (optional)

Directions

Drain the red kidney beans, but not the black beans. Combine all ingredients in a large pot and place on the stovetop over medium heat. Stir clockwise as you envision the element of Fire resonating and expanding within the chili. You might imagine a single flame or the flames of a bonfire. You might imagine the hot, golden sunlight radiating off the desert sands. Create a symbol or a scene in your mind to represent fire, heat, and light. Make your imaginations as vivid as possible, and use these visualizations every time you stir the chili. Add fully cooked meat or plant-based protein if desired. Heat for about 15 or 20 minutes, until bell pepper pieces are tender and onion pieces are translucent.

General notes

SPICY FIRE TOFU TACOS

Effects: Eat to clear obstacles, strengthen defenses, and boost resolve.

Makes: 4 to 6 servings

Ingredients

1 block tofu, extra-firm	1 tsp garlic powder
1 C flour	Onion
¼ C cornstarch	Hot sauce
Vegetable oil for frying	Shredded cheese
1–2 tbsp soy sauce	Shredded lettuce
½ tsp cumin	Crunchy taco shells or
1 tsp chili powder	soft tortillas

Directions

Gently squeeze the tofu to remove as much water as possible and then pat it dry. Cut it into 1-inch cubes. As you pass the knife smoothly through the tofu, imagine easily getting through any obstacles. Mix the flour and cornstarch in a large bowl, then gently toss the tofu cubes in the mixture to coat them on all sides. If you prefer, you can substitute rice flour in place of the regular flour and cornstarch. Imagine the tofu cubes are little bricks or stones you can use to build a fortress. Fry the cubes in a quarter- to a half-inch of vegetable oil over medium-high heat, about 1 to 2 minutes on each side or until golden brown. Kitchen tongs work well for handling the tofu in the oil. Remove the tofu from the oil, then place in a bowl or serving dish and douse with soy sauce. Shake the container gently to distribute the soy sauce, then sprinkle the tofu generously with all the spices. Think of the heat of the spices going into the tofu as you add each one, imagining the power and flavor that each ingredient is bringing. Imagine flames dancing throughout the container as you gently shake it around again to distribute the spices. You can use the filling for tacos or burritos. Top with chopped onion, hot sauce, shredded cheese, shredded lettuce, or any other desired condiments.

General notes

_____

_____

_____

_____

_____

_____

_____

_____

_____

HOT CINNAMON COCOA

Effects: Drink to encourage passion and increase energy.
Makes: 2 servings

Ingredients

2½ C milk or water

2 tbsp sugar

1 tbsp cocoa powder

1 tsp cinnamon

1 cinnamon stick

Whipped cream (optional)

Directions

Heat milk or water over low to medium heat until steam begins to rise. Stir in sugar, cocoa powder, and powdered cinnamon. Whisk vigorously until combined. Pour into drinking cups. Stir in a triangular pattern with a cinnamon stick and imagine a campfire or candle flame. Think of the fluid motion and vibrant energy of flame as you stir the cocoa. Top with whipped cream if desired.

Water

The element of water is associated with life, creation, cleansing, love, and healing. It encompasses the power of all the water on earth. Water can transform, refresh, nurture, quench, satisfy, enthrall, and enchant. Use the water element in your diet to increase vitality, encourage calmness, spark creativity, invite love, inspire compassion, encourage cooperation, build friendships, and support healing. Water also acts as a blank slate, capable of being imprinted with whatever energies one chooses to impart upon it. Air-aligned foods pair well energetically with water-aligned foods, enhancing the transforming, refreshing qualities of water. When using water-aligned foods or cooking techniques, envision a cool, refreshing stream, nourishing rain, a romantic waterfall, a powerful ocean, an unstoppable river carving through the landscape. Think of what you wish your magick to accomplish, and think of how the element of water encapsulates this idea.

Cooking Methods

Washing, steaming, boiling, poaching.

Ingredients

In addition to water itself, other water-aligned ingredients include vegetables and fruits with high water content as well as foods that are harvested in or near a body of water. Foods that are eaten when young and fresh, foods that are aligned with lunar energies, and foods associated with the sea, love, and fertility are also included.

Celery	Nori
Cherries	Olives
Cranberries	Peaches
Cucumbers	Pears
Grapes	Poppy seeds
Ice cream	Sea salt
Kiwi	Snow peas
Lettuce	Sprouts
Mango	Sweet peas
Melons	Water chestnuts
Mint	Watercress

COOLING CUCUMBER APPETIZER

· ·

Effects: Eat to encourage feelings of calm and relaxation.

Makes: 4 servings

Ingredients

2 medium cucumbers

Small pinch of salt (about ¼ tsp)

½ C plain Greek yogurt

1 tsp lemon juice

1 tsp dill

¼ C bean sprouts

Directions

Cut the cucumbers into ¼-inch thick rounds and sprinkle lightly with salt. Hold your hand over the cucumbers as you think of the ocean waves gently rolling in and out. Mix together the yogurt, lemon juice, and dill. Place a small dollop of the yogurt mixture on each cucumber round, and top with a pinch of bean sprouts. The yogurt mixture also makes a good vegetable dip to serve with celery sticks or other fresh veggies.

JUICY FRUIT SALAD

Effects: Eat to encourage feelings of love and
compassion.

Makes: 4 to 6 servings

Ingredients

3 peaches   2 C whipped cream

2 pears   1 tbsp honey (optional)

2 C cherries

Directions

Peel the peaches and cut them into bite-sized pieces. Peel
the pears and dice into small pieces, about half the size of
the peach pieces. If the cherries have pits, cut them in half
and remove the pits. Mix all the fruit together in a large
bowl as you envision the fruits growing on the trees, and
think of the water the trees drew up from the ground to
flow throughout the branches and into the fruit. Think of
the unique essence of each of the fruits as you mix them
together, and think also of their similarities. Serve the
fruit mixture in small bowls, and top each serving with a
dollop of the whipped cream. Drizzle a little honey onto
the whipped cream if desired.

COOL WATER SALAD

Effects: Eat for inspiration and to boost creative energy.

Makes: 2 to 4 servings

Ingredients

4 C green leaf lettuce

¼ C water chestnuts

¼ C olives

1 stalk celery

¼ C olive oil

1 tbsp lemon juice

¼ tsp sea salt

Directions

Chop or tear the green leaf lettuce into bite-sized pieces. Mince the water chestnuts and slice or chop the olives. Scrape the stringy ribs from the celery, then dice it into very small pieces. Combine the water chestnuts, celery, olives, and lettuce in a large bowl. In a separate bowl, stir together the olive oil, lemon juice, and sea salt. Drizzle this over the salad, pouring about half of it on to start. Stir the salad with a fork to evenly distribute the dressing, and add more to your preference. As you mix it all together, think of all the variety of water on earth—streams, rivers, ponds, oceans, lakes, glaciers: as many as you can think of to get your thoughts flowing toward the flow of water. Invite the energies of the water element into the salad.

Air

The element of air represents the winds, the atmosphere, the breath, the realm of thought, and the substance of spirit. Air animates and moves things, and it can also refresh, cool off, and change things. Air can blow things away or bring things toward you. It is the element of movement and the ruler of the fresh and new. Incorporate air-attuned ingredients in your recipes to refresh the mind and spirit, encourage communication and eloquence, speed things along, boost the intellect, support safe and happy travels, transform a situation, or ease a change. You can also use air-aligned ingredients in combination with fire-attuned herbs to add a boost of power to banishing magick. When using air-aligned ingredients and cooking techniques, envision a strong wind or a gentle breeze flowing into the food, blowing into it your magickal intention.

Cooking Techniques

Whipping, aerating, air frying, drying, techniques that incorporate air like making tempuras and souffles.

Ingredients

Herbs with a light scent, plants with a delicate, airy structure, and plants that are said to be ruled by the planet Mercury are attuned with the air element.

Almond	Lavender
Beans	Lemongrass
Caraway	Marjoram
Carbonated beverages	Mint
Cilantro	Parsley
Dill	Sage
Fennel	Tofu
Flax	Whipped cream

General notes

_____

_____

_____

_____

_____

_____

_____

_____

_____

TOFU TEMPURA
WITH MARJORAM
• •

Effects: Eat to inspire change or encourage action.
Makes: 4 to 6 servings

Ingredients

1 block extra-firm tofu	½ tsp salt
Cooking oil	1¾ C club soda, chilled
¾ C all-purpose flour	½ tsp marjoram
½ C rice flour	½ tsp dill

For dipping sauce

½ C sour cream	1 tbsp dill
2 tbsp marjoram	Salt to taste

Directions

Drain the tofu and gently squeeze the block on all sides, removing as much water as possible. Cut the tofu block in half vertically, then slice it horizontally into ¼-inch-thick slices. Heat a deep pan on the stove over medium-high heat, filling it about ¼–½ inch deep with cooking oil. Next, mix together the flours and salt, then add the cold club soda (Note: make sure the club soda is very cold.) Stir the batter gently just enough to incorporate everything; you don't want to overmix it. As you stir, imagine the wind whirling through the bubbly batter. Think of the action or changes you would like to see in your life. The batter should be bubbly. Gently dip the pieces of tofu into the tempura batter. Let most of the excess drip off, then place the tofu in the hot oil, cooking in small batches. Fry for about 30 seconds on each side. For the dipping sauce, combine the sour cream, marjoram, and dill; add salt to taste and stir until blended.

General notes

_____

_____

_____

_____

_____

_____

_____

_____

_____

_____

_____

_____

_____

_____

_____

_____

_____

PARSLEY CREAM PASTA
· ·

Effects: Eat to banish stale energies and feel refreshed.
Makes: 4 servings

Ingredients

8 oz. fresh or dried pasta (linguine or spaghetti work well)

1 bunch parsley

¼ C olive oil

¼ C almonds, chopped or slivered

½ C milk

⅛–¼ tsp salt

Additional slivered almonds for garnish (optional)

Directions

Add the pasta to a large pot of salted, boiling water. Chop the parsley, removing the stems and any discolored leaves. As you trim and chop the parsley, think of weeding out the stale energies from your life. In a blender or food processor, mix the olive oil, almonds, parsley, milk, and about ⅛ to ¼ tsp salt. Pulse the blender until well-blended into a puree. As you blend the ingredients, imagine a fresh breeze blowing over you. Envision the new energies you want to welcome into your life. Pour the puree into a small saucepan and heat over medium-low heat, stirring occasionally. Drain the pasta once it's tender, then top with the parsley cream sauce. Garnish with additional slivered almonds if desired.

SAGE SOUFFLE

· ·

Effects: Eat to bring wisdom and to encourage good
communication.

Makes: 4 servings

Ingredients

4 eggs

1 C milk

2 tbsp butter

2 tbsp flour

¼ tsp salt

1 tsp sage

½ C cheese

1 tbsp butter for
ramekins

¼ C breadcrumbs for
ramekins

Directions

Set the eggs out until they warm to room temperature
to ensure best results. Preheat the oven to 400° F. Crack
the eggs and separate the yolks from the whites. Collect the egg whites in a dry metal bowl, and make sure
your whisk is dry. Whip the egg whites rapidly with the
whisk for about 3 to 5 minutes, until soft peaks form.
As you whisk the egg whites, imagine the wind whipping through them, transforming their structure. Heat
the milk over low heat in a saucepan on the stove. You
want it to reach steaming hot but not boiling. In another
pan, melt 2 tbsp of butter over medium heat, then add
in 2 tbsp of flour, stirring it together to create a thick

roux. Add the warm milk to the roux a little at a time, whisking constantly until all the milk is incorporated and the mixture has achieved a smooth texture without any lumps. Remove from the heat and let the mixture cool. Then whisk in the egg yolks one at a time. Stir in the salt, sage, and cheese. You'll need 4 small ramekins. Grease the ramekins with butter and coat with breadcrumbs, tapping out the excess. Gently fold the egg yolk mixture into the egg whites, then spoon into the prepared ramekins, filling each cup about ⅔ to ¾ full. Bake at 400 degrees for about 5 minutes, then turn the oven down to 350 and bake for an additional 15 to 20 minutes, depending on the size of the souffles. The souffles should poof up and be golden brown on top but slightly jiggly. Serve immediately, as souffles quickly deflate after leaving the oven.

Earth

The element of earth represents the power of the land, the mountains, the soil, the plains. It encompasses the strength of stone and the growth of vegetation and animalia. Incorporate into your meals ingredients associated with the earth element to boost protection, gain strength, support tenacity, promote growth, or bring prosperity and abundance. The earth element is grounding, balancing, sustaining, and strengthening. It brings added power when used with fire-aligned ingredients, and it can add an additional layer of settling, soothing energies when used with water-aligned ingredients. Combined with air-aligned ingredients, earth-attuned foods can help forge a stronger connection. The earth element is associated with the underworld as well as the spirit realm and rules the gate between the living and the dead. Some earth-aligned ingredients, such as mushrooms, pomegranates, and apples can help facilitate both giving and receiving messages from loved ones who have passed away. When incorporating the earth element in your cooking, think of your specific goal and then visualize how the earth reflects it. For instance, if your goal is prosperity, think of all the fruits of Nature, from the actual fruit on the trees to the abundant grasses and grain. Imagine the food you are cooking as the earth itself, then envision in it whatever qualities you are going for: blossoming with greenery for prosperity, growth, or abundance, turning into impenetrable solid stone for strength and stability, transforming into a fertile field for foundation or opportunity.

Cooking Techniques

Using metal, stone, or pottery cookware; pit cooking, baking, roasting.

Ingredients

Earth-aligned foods include tubers that grow underground; dark leafy greens; foods with a rich, savory, or hearty flavor; and foods with a meaty, mealy, or grainy texture. Foods that grow on prickly or thorny plants, plants that produce an abundance of fruits or seeds, grains, and foods associated with agricultural deities are also aligned with the earth element.

Apples	Carrots
Blackberries	Cocoa

Collard greens

Corn

Cumin

Garlic

Ginger

Honey

Kale

Maple syrup

Mushrooms

Mustard

Nutmeg

Onions

Oregano

Pecans

Pomegranate

Potatoes

Saffron

Salt

Sesame

Spinach

Squash

Turmeric

Walnuts

Wheat

General notes

_____

_____

_____

_____

_____

_____

_____

_____

_____

STRENGTHENING
SESAME STIR FRY
• •

Effects: Eat to increase strength and promote stamina.

Makes: 4 servings

Ingredients

2 chicken breasts or
    one block extra firm
    tofu

1 C flour

¼ C cornstarch

1 tsp salt

Vegetable oil for frying

2 cloves garlic

1 bunch kale

1 small onion

⅛ C soy sauce

1 tbsp plus 1 tsp sesame
    oil

2 tbsp sesame seeds

¼ tsp red pepper flakes

¼ tsp ginger

Directions

Depending on your choice of chicken or tofu, begin by trimming the fat and skin from the chicken, or gently squeeze the water out of the tofu. Cut the tofu or chicken into small, bite-sized pieces. Mix together the flour, cornstarch, and 1 tsp salt, and toss the tofu or chicken in this mixture until the pieces are lightly dusted. Heat about ¼–½ inch of vegetable oil on the stove in a large pan on medium high heat until the oil is sizzling hot. Add the tofu or chicken in small batches, cooking on each side for about 2 to 3 minutes until golden brown. If you're cooking chicken, cut a piece in half to be sure it's cooked throughout. While the chicken or tofu cooks, mince the garlic and chop the kale into large pieces. The kale will shrink as it cooks, so you can keep the pieces fairly large. Slice the onion into thin slices. Heat 2 tbsp vegetable oil in a large pan or wok. Stir fry the kale, minced garlic, and onion for about one minute, until it becomes aromatic and the kale begins to shrink, then mix in the cooked chicken or tofu. Add the soy sauce, sesame oil, ginger, and red pepper flakes. Stir to incorporate, and heat for a couple more minutes, stirring gently and frequently. As the food cooks, imagine the strength of the earth, the hardness of stone, the power of the land. Sprinkle with sesame seeds to finish.

General notes

_____

_____

_____

_____

_____

_____

GROUNDING STEW

Effects: Eat to help ground and stabilize after a hectic or stressful day.

Makes: 4 servings

Ingredients

1 onion

5 carrots

5 potatoes

2 tbsp butter

¼ tsp salt

¼ tsp pepper

2 tsp garlic

2 10.5-oz. cans condensed cream of mushroom soup

1–2 C milk (or water)

Directions

Dice the onion and chop the carrots and potatoes into bite-size pieces. Boil the carrots and potatoes until tender, then drain. Sauté the onion in the butter, seasoning with the salt, pepper, and garlic. Then combine with the carrots, potatoes, and the condensed cream of mushroom soup. Cooked beef, cooked chicken, or plant-based beef or chicken substitute can be added if desired. Add 1 to 2 C milk or water to thin the stew to suit your preference. Trace a pentacle shape in the stew as you mix it.

FRIED MUSHROOMS

Effects: Eat prior to communicating with the dead to help you be more receptive to messages.

Makes: 4 servings

Ingredients

1 C flour

½ tsp salt

¼ C cornstarch

1 tsp baking soda

1¼ C milk or water

8 oz. white button mushrooms

Vegetable oil

For dipping sauce

3 tbsp mustard

2 tbsp honey

4 tbsp mayonnaise

¼ tsp pepper

Directions

Mix together the flour, salt, cornstarch, baking soda, and milk or water to make a batter. Heat the oil in a pan, making sure the oil is at least ½ inch deep. Dip each mushroom in the batter, letting the excess drip back down into the bowl. Gently place in the oil and fry until golden brown, about 1 minute on each side. Think of loved ones who have passed away as you fry the mushrooms. Think of the ephemeral nature of mushrooms and humans alike. Mix together the mustard, honey, mayonnaise, and pepper to create a dipping sauce.

General notes

_____

_____

_____

_____

_____

_____

_____

_____

_____

_____

_____

_____

_____

_____

_____

_____

_____

_____

_____

_____

_____

_____

_____

_____

General notes

Section 4

Celestial
Cooking

Celestial cooking is much like cooking with the elements, only the ingredient alignments are not based on the attributes of the earthly elements, but rather on the attributes and influences of the sun, moon, and planets that occupy our solar system.

Moon

Lunar energies are associated with the psychic, emotional, and spiritual realms. Ingredients associated with the moon include fruits and vegetables sacred to lunar goddesses, foods that have a sweet or mellow flavor, foods that are white or round, foods associated with the underworld or afterlife, and foods associated with the water element. Use lunar-attuned ingredients to increase psychic awareness, encourage prophetic dreams, invite inspiration, attract love, encourage healing, bring wisdom, or honor the dead.

Apples	Cherries
Apricots	Coconut
Bananas	Cucumbers
Cabbage	Grapes
Cannabis	Lemons

Lettuce

Mushrooms

Olives

Plums

Pomegranate

Poppy seeds

Papaya

Pears

Peaches

Peas

Potatoes

Turnip

Water chestnut

Watercress

Vanilla

General notes

_____

_____

_____

_____

_____

_____

_____

_____

_____

_____

_____

_____

_____

LEMON AND
POPPY LUNAR THINS

Effects: Eat to enhance psychic abilities or encourage prophetic dreams.

Makes: 4 to 6 servings

Ingredients

½ C butter (1 stick)

½ C white sugar

½ C brown sugar

1 egg

1½ tsp vanilla extract

1 tsp lemon extract

2 lemons

1 C flour

1½ tsp baking powder

⅛ tsp salt

¼–½ tsp poppy seeds

For optional icing

1 C powdered sugar

Juice from 1 lemon

¼ tsp vanilla extract

Directions

Preheat the oven to 350° F. Set the butter out to soften before you begin. Mash together the butter, white sugar, and brown sugar. Add the egg, vanilla extract, and lemon extract. Zest both lemons, and add the zest from both to the sugar and butter mixture. Collect the juice from one of the lemons and mix this in, as well.

In a separate bowl, combine the flour, baking powder, and salt. Then pour the flour mixture into the butter and sugar mixture, and gently fold the ingredients together until combined into a dough. As you mix the dough, envision moonlight streaming into the bowl. Think of the energies of the lemon resonating throughout the mixture.

Scoop out one to two tablespoons of the dough at a time and roll into a ball. Pat the ball to flatten it into a disc, ¼ to ½ inches in thickness. Place the cookies at least 3 to 4 inches apart on a greased cookie sheet. Sprinkle poppy seeds onto the cookies as you think of your psychic senses opening. Bake for 12 to 15 minutes.

For crispier cookies, use only one tablespoon of dough for each cookie and flatten them to just over ¼ inch thick. Bake a little longer until the cookies are crisp and brown around the edges. For a softer cookie, use 2 tbsp of dough per cookie and flatten them to ½ inch thick. Cook a little less, just until the tops look done.

As the cookies cool, make the icing. Combine 1 C powdered sugar with the juice from the other lemon, along with ¼ tsp vanilla extract. If possible, mix the icing outside under the moonlight and invite the moon's energies to enter the mixture as you stir it. Once the cookies have cooled completely, top each one with a dollop of the icing and spread it around with the back of a spoon. Sprinkle additional poppy seeds on top of the icing if desired.

MOON-ATTUNED
MUSHROOMS
. . . .

Effects: Eat to bring inspiration, enhance beauty and
magnetism, and heighten psychic awareness.

Makes: 4 to 6 servings

Ingredients

8 oz. white button
mushrooms

2 cloves garlic

2 tbsp olive oil, divided

½ C black olives

½ C grated parmesan
cheese

Directions

Wash the mushrooms, then gently twist the stems to remove
them. Peel the garlic cloves. Mince the mushroom stems
and the garlic. Heat 1 tbsp of the olive oil over medium high
heat. Add the mushroom stem
pieces and the garlic, and cook
for about 30 seconds, just
until tender and fragrant.
Put the stem pieces and
garlic in a small bowl, then
add one more tablespoon of
olive oil to the hot pan. Add the
mushroom caps, cooking for about
15 seconds on each side. Place the mush-

room caps on a baking pan with their undersides facing upward. Mix the stem pieces and garlic with the parmesan cheese. For a vegan version, substitute finely diced tomatoes for the cheese. Fill each mushroom cap with about 2 tsp of mushroom stem mixture, then top with a whole olive resting on its side. Hold your hand over the mushrooms and think about the moon. Invite these lunar energies to enchant the mushrooms. Broil in the oven for 1 to 3 minutes until the cheese melts and the olives warm.

General notes

_____

_____

_____

_____

_____

_____

_____

_____

_____

_____

_____

_____

CHERRY
LUNAR LEMONADE

Effects: Drink to attract love and increase passion.

Makes: 1 serving

Ingredients

¾ C cold water ¼ C cherry juice

2 lemons, juiced 1–2 tbsp sugar

Directions

Pour the cold water into a glass, then add the juice from the lemons. As you stir in the lemon juice, imagine moonlight shining into the mixture. Add the cherry juice. This drink can be made either sweet or tart. Just stir in the sugar a little at a time and taste as you go to get the right amount to suit your preference.

Sun

The sun is associated with energy, light, warmth, and life. Solar-aligned foods tend to have a very positive and vibrant energy, and many of these ingredients have an orange or yellow hue. Foods associated with the sun are often also associated with the fire element. Use solar-attuned foods to bring success, inspire joy, enhance magickal power, boost vitality and strength, illuminate the hidden, and encourage growth.

Basil	Pineapple
Bay	Red pepper flakes
Chili powder	Rice
Cinnamon	Rosemary
Corn	Saffron
Cornmeal	Salt
Ginger	Sesame
Grains	Strawberries
Grapefruit	Sunflower seeds
Limes	Tangerine
Olives	Tea
Oranges	Tomatoes
Peppers	

SUN TEA
· · · · · · · · · · · · · · · ·

Effects: Drink to encourage cheerfulness, success, growth, and confidence.

Makes: 4 servings

Ingredients

4 tea bags, individual
serving size

Half gallon water

1 tsp cinnamon powder

¼ C sugar (optional)

Directions

This recipe is to be made on a hot, sunny day. Place the tea bags and water in a clear glass container and close or cover securely. Place the container outside in a place where it will receive direct sunlight. Feel the sun's warmth and invite the rays of sunshine to enter the container and imbue your tea with solar power. Leave the container outside for a few hours. Remove the tea bags, then add the cinnamon powder and optional sugar, stirring vigorously to blend it in and further energize the mixture. If sunny, warm weather isn't the norm where you live, you can heat the water on the stove or in the microwave and set the tea near a window for a few minutes to get the sunlight. Refrigerate until cool and serve over ice if desired.

SUNSHINE CORNBREAD

Effects: Eat to invite happiness, growth, and success.
Makes: 4 to 6 servings

Ingredients

¾ C cornmeal

1¼ C all-purpose flour

¼ tsp salt

½ C sugar

1–2 tsp fresh or dried basil

3 mandarin oranges

¼ C oil

1 egg

½ C milk

1½ tsp baking powder

For the glaze

Orange scraps

3 tbsp water

1½ tbsp sugar

¼ tsp cinnamon

Directions

Place the basil and cinnamon in the sunlight for a few minutes before you begin. Preheat the oven to 350° F. In a large mixing bowl, combine the cornmeal, flour, salt, sugar, and basil. Zest and juice three mandarin oranges. In total, you should get about 1 tbsp of zest and ⅓ C of juice. After you juice the oranges, put the squeezed and zested orange remnants in a small saucepan. Add 3 tbsp water, 1½ tbsp sugar, and ¼ tsp cinnamon. This will become the glaze, but don't start it cooking just yet. Turn your attention back to the cornbread and stir in the orange juice and zest. Think about the sun's warmth and how it supports life and growth. Then add the ¼ C of oil and one egg. Measure out the milk, and stir into it the 1½ tsp baking powder. Add it to the batter and mix just until incorporated. Put the batter in a greased round baking pan and bake for about 20 minutes or until the cornbread is cooked all the way through. While the cornbread cools, begin the glaze: Turn the heat to medium and stir the mixture frequently, pressing down on the orange remnants to extract the juices. Let it cook for about five minutes. Once it has cooled slightly, press out as much liquid as you can from the pieces of orange, then discard them. Drizzle the glaze over the top of the cornbread, using the back of a spoon to spread the glaze over the top of the loaf.

General notes

_____

_____

_____

_____

FRIED CHICKEN OR TOFU
WITH ORANGE SAUCE

• •

Effects: Eat to boost personal power, strength, and
confidence.

Makes: 4 servings

Ingredients

2–3 boneless chicken
breasts or 1 block
extra-firm tofu

1 C flour

½–¾ tsp salt

¼ C cornstarch for
coating

1 egg

1 C milk

Cooking oil for frying

2 C rice (optional)

For the Sauce

1 C orange juice

1 tsp soy sauce

1 tsp garlic

½ tsp ginger

⅛–¼ tsp red pepper
flakes

¼ C hot water

1½ tbsp cornstarch

1 tbsp sugar

Directions

Drain the tofu or trim the chicken, depending on your
choice of protein. If using tofu, place the block between
your palms and apply even pressure with your whole hands
to gently squeeze out as much moisture from the tofu block

as possible. Cut the tofu or chicken into 1-inch cubes. Combine the flour, ½ tsp salt, and ¼ C of cornstarch. In a small bowl, whisk together the egg and the milk.

If you're making rice to go with your meal, begin cooking it now according to package directions or your favorite method. (One way is to use twice as much water as rice, bring to a boil, then reduce heat, cover, and simmer until water is absorbed, about 15 to 20 minutes).

Fill a deep pan on the stove with about a half-inch of oil and heat it over medium-high heat. Place a handful of tofu or chicken in the dry flour mixture, and toss to coat. Next, dip the pieces in the egg and milk, then put them back in the bowl of flour. Toss to coat the tofu or chicken with the flour. Fry in small batches of 6 to 10 pieces at a time in the hot oil, about 1 to 2 minutes each side for tofu, and about 2 to 3 minutes each side for chicken. If you're cooking chicken, test for doneness by cutting one of the largest pieces in half to make sure it is cooked all the way through, no pink. As you fry the chicken or tofu, heat in a separate pan or pot over medium-low heat the orange juice, soy sauce, garlic, ginger, and red pepper flakes. Add a small sprinkling of salt. Place 1 tbsp cornstarch in a ¼ C measuring cup, and add hot water to nearly fill the cup. Stir the contents to dissolve the cornstarch, then add this liquid to the orange juice mixture. Continue simmering the sauce, stirring occasionally, until it thickens. As you stir the sauce, envision a strong lion walking around in the sunshine, the golden light warming its fur. Serve the sauce over the fried tofu or chicken, along with a side of rice if desired.

Mercury

Mercury is associated with intelligence, direction, and refinement. Use Mercury-attuned ingredients to encourage movement, wisdom, speed, victory, eloquence, smooth communication, and grace.

Almonds	Lemongrass
Caraway	Mace
Carrots	Marjoram
Celery	Mint
Dill	Oats
Fennel	Parsley
Flax	Parsnips
Lavender	Thyme

PARSNIPS AND CARROTS
WITH TOASTED ALMONDS

Effects: Eat to encourage wisdom and honest, productive communication.

Makes: 6 to 8 servings

Ingredients

1 lb. parsnips

1 lb. carrots

2 tbsp cooking oil

1 tsp thyme

1 tsp salt

1 tbsp dried parsley

1 tsp fennel

½ C almond slivers

1 tbsp butter

Directions

Preheat the oven to 350° F. Peel the parsnips and cut off the ends. Then cut them into two-inch chunks. Stand each chunk on its end and use a paring knife to carefully cut strips of the parsnip from around the woody center core. Discard the core, and cut the parsnip strips into smaller, bite-sized pieces. Cut the carrots into ½-inch pieces. Place the vegetables in a baking pan and toss with the cooking oil. Add the thyme, salt, parsley, and fennel, mixing to distribute the seasonings. Sprinkle on a layer of almond slivers. Invite the energies of Mercury to be prominent in the dish. Bake for about 25 minutes, until carrots and parsnips are tender. Pierce 1 tbsp butter on the end of a fork and rub it over the hot vegetables to coat them.

CELERY CREAM SOUP
WITH LAVENDER

Effects: Eat to end delays and get things moving quickly in the right direction.

Makes: 2 servings

Ingredients

4 stalks celery

1 C milk

1 C heavy cream

¼ tsp salt

½ tsp dried (or 1 tsp fresh) lavender flowers, plus more for garnish

¼ tsp dill weed

Directions

Trim the ends off the celery, then cut each stalk lengthwise down the middle. Then cut the celery into thin slices about ¼ inch thick. Put 1 C of the celery in a food processor with 1 C of milk. Blend until pureed. Add this to a pot along with the heavy cream, salt, and remaining celery. Cook over medium low heat for about 8 minutes, then add the ½ tsp dried lavender flowers and the dill. Imagine things in your life going smoothly and any desired actions happening swiftly. Reduce the heat to low and cook for an additional 5 to 8 minutes. Ladle into individual bowls, then top each bowl with a light sprinkling of lavender.

Venus

Venus is associated with love, desire, passion, optimism, fertility, creation, and nourishment. Use recipes aligned with Venus to encourage loving feelings and friendship, renew hope, manifest abundance, or bring growth.

Apples

Apricots

Artichokes

Avocados

Bananas

Barley

Basil

Blackberries

Cardamom

Cherries

Figs

Mint

Olives

Plums

Peaches

Pears

Peas

Strawberries

Thyme

Tomatoes

Raspberries

Vanilla

Wheat

ARTICHOKE CREAM POT PIE

Effects: Share with loved ones to encourage feelings of love and harmony.

Makes: 6 servings

Ingredients

1 12–16-oz. can artichoke hearts

8 oz. cream cheese

¼ C mayonnaise

1 C shredded mozzarella cheese

1 tsp basil

¼ tsp salt

1 tsp olive oil

For pie crust

1¼ C flour

¼ tsp salt

1 stick cold butter

¼ C cold water

Directions

Preheat the oven to 350° F. Begin by preparing the pie crust. Mix together the flour and salt. Cut the butter into ⅛-inch-thick slivers and add to the flour, using a pastry blender or the back of a fork to cut in the butter. You can also use your clean, dry hands, grabbing pinches of the mixture between your fingers and making a pinching and twisting motion to blend it together. You want it to be the consistency of wet, crumbly sand with some bigger chunks of butter still visible. Then add the cold water a tablespoon at a time, mixing gently until the dough comes together. Gently knead the dough just enough to form it into a cohesive mass, then let it chill in the refrigerator for about an hour. If you prefer, you can use a readymade refrigerated pie crust dough.

Once the pie crust dough has chilled, set the cream cheese out to soften for a few minutes. Roll out the pie crust dough on a floured surface using a floured rolling pin, until it's an ⅛ inch thick at most. Put the dough into a greased pie pan, pushing it in place to cover the bottom and sides of the pan. Prick the bottom of the crust a few times with a fork, then bake it for about 13 to 15 minutes or until it no longer looks raw and doughy. Next, mash together the cream cheese, mayonnaise, basil, and salt. Drain and rinse the artichoke hearts, then blend them in with the cream cheese mixture, along with the shredded mozzarella cheese. Invite the energies of Venus to enchant the food. Pour the mixture in the pie crust. Bake in the oven for 25 to 30 minutes, until the crust is golden and the top is firm.

BROWN SUGARED
APRICOTS WITH CARDAMOM

Effects: Eat to enhance beauty, encourage passion, or support healing.

Makes: 4 to 6 servings

Ingredients

2 cans apricots (or 8–10 fresh)

¼–½ C brown sugar

2 tsp ground cardamom

2 tbsp butter

Whipped cream (optional)

Directions

Preheat oven to 350° F. If using canned apricots, drain and rinse the fruit. If you're using fresh apricots, peel them, slice into halves, and remove the pits. Place the apricots in a bowl and sprinkle over them the brown sugar and cardamom. Toss the fruit to evenly distribute the sugar and spices. Think about the essence of the apricots becoming intertwined with the energies of the cardamom. Next arrange the apricots in a single layer in a buttered baking dish. Cut 2 tbsp of butter into thin slivers, and arrange the butter pieces on top of the apricots. Bake for about 10 minutes for canned apricots or about 20–25 minutes for fresh apricots. Serve with whipped cream and a sprinkle of extra cardamom, if desired.

Mars

Mars has a strong, aggressive energy that can be either stabilizing or destructive. Make use of Mars-aligned ingredients and recipes to strengthen defenses; bolster protection; increase courage; and boost ambition, confidence, power, or tenacity. Mars ingredients can also be used for purification and banishing.

Allspice

Basil

Black pepper

Chili powder

Chilies

Cumin

Garlic

Horseradish

Jalapeños

Mustard

Onions

Paprika

Peppers

Radishes

Red beans

Red bell pepper

Red pepper flakes

White pepper

SPICY HOT ONION RINGS
WITH RED PEPPER SAUCE

Effects: Eat to gain strength and courage, and for luck
and extra power in overcoming enemies.

Makes: 3 to 4 servings

Ingredients

2 large onions	1 tsp black pepper
1 C flour	1 tsp paprika
½ tsp salt, divided	1 tsp chili powder
1½ C beer or club soda	Cooking oil for frying

For sauce

½ C mayonnaise	1 tsp paprika
2–3 tsp red pepper flakes	½–1 tsp chili powder
	½ tsp garlic powder

Directions

Peel the onions and cut them into ¼–½-inch thick rings.
Mix together the flour and ¼ tsp salt. Heat about ½ inch
of oil in a deep pan on high heat. Add the beer or club soda
to the flour mixture and stir to make a batter. It should
be fairly thin, like pancake batter. Dip the onion rings in
the batter, then place them a few at a time in the hot oil.
They will cook quickly, in just about 30 seconds on each
side. Imagine breaking through brick walls with ease as

you fry the onion rings. Use a pair of kitchen tongs to flip them over and remove them from the oil. Drain on paper towels or on a wire rack. Sprinkle the onion rings with an additional ¼ tsp salt, along with 1 tsp black pepper, 1 tsp paprika, and 1 tsp chili powder. To make the dipping sauce, mix together the mayonnaise, red pepper flakes, paprika, chili powder, and garlic powder. Use the maximum suggested amounts of red pepper flakes and chili powder for a spicier sauce, and stick with the lesser suggested amounts for a mild sauce with a subtle afterbite that builds.

General notes

_____

_____

_____

_____

_____

_____

_____

_____

_____

_____

_____

MARS POWER TACOS

. . . .

Effects: Eat to boost defenses and increase personal
   power and strength.

Makes: 4 servings

Ingredients

2 boneless chicken
   breasts or 4 large
   potatoes

Cooking oil

4 tsp paprika

2 tsp chili powder

¼ tsp black pepper

½ tsp salt

1 red bell pepper

1–3 jalapeños

Butter or oil for
   sautéing

Crunchy taco shells or
   heated corn tortillas

Your favorite taco
   toppings

Directions

Choose chicken or potatoes to be the star of this dish. If
using chicken, cut the meat into 1-inch pieces. If potatoes
are your choice, cut each potato in half lengthwise, then
horizontal. Cut each segment vertically
down the middle, then cut into
¼-inch-thick slices. Heat some
cooking oil in a pan on the stovetop
at medium-high heat. Use only a
tablespoon of oil if you're cooking
chicken; for potatoes, you'll want

the oil to fill the pan about ½ inch deep. Whether cooking chicken or potatoes, fry it in small batches so that the pan is not overcrowded. Chicken will take around 2 to 3 minutes each side, and potatoes will take around 3 to 5 minutes each side. Once the pieces have finished cooking, remove from the oil and transfer to another dish. Sprinkle on them the paprika, chili powder, black pepper, and salt. Invite the energies of Mars to enchant the food as you sprinkle on the spices. Next, slice the red bell pepper into thin strips and dice the jalapeño. Sauté these in a small amount of butter or oil until fragrant and vibrant. Fill each tortilla or shell with a mixture of the chicken or potatoes topped with the bell pepper and jalapeños. Add any other toppings you like, such as chopped onion, shredded cheese, or hot sauce.

24

Jupiter

Jupiter is associated with luck, expansion, growth, justice, wisdom, and success. Use Jupiter-attuned foods to attract prosperity and good fortune, open new opportunities, bring about justice, invite wisdom, or increase the chance for success.

Anise	Oregano
Asparagus	Raisins
Basil	Sage
Bell peppers	Star anise
Clove	Tomatoes
Currants	Turmeric
Ginger	Turnips
Maple syrup	Vanilla
Nutmeg	Yellow squash

NUTMEG VANILLA CREPES

Effects: Eat to invite good luck and bring success.

Makes: 3 to 4 servings

Ingredients

1 C flour	2 tbsp sugar
1 C milk	Butter
2 eggs	Whipped cream
½ tsp nutmeg	Maple syrup
1 tsp vanilla extract	

Directions

Mix together the flour, milk, eggs, nutmeg, vanilla extract, and sugar. Melt about a tablespoon of butter in a large pan on the stove over medium-high heat. Pour a small amount (¼ C or less) of the crepe batter into the pan, then either tilt the pan in different directions, or use the back of a tablespoon to quickly spread out the batter in a wide, very thin layer that nearly covers the pan. Let the crepe cook for about 40 to 45 seconds, then flip and cook an additional 5 to 10 seconds. Transfer the crepe to a plate. Put a line of whipped cream across the middle of the crepe, then roll it toward yourself to bring in good luck. Imagine the success you want happening as you roll the crepes. Top with a drizzle of maple syrup before serving.

OVEN-FRIED PEPPERS WITH TURMERIC BUTTER SAUCE

Effects: Eat to boost luck, encourage confidence, and invite good fortune.

Makes: 2 to 4 servings

Ingredients

Vegetable oil

1 bell pepper, yellow or orange

¼ C flour

½ C panko crumbs

1 egg

¼ tsp salt

¼ tsp oregano

For Sauce

¾–1 C milk

2 tbsp butter

2 tbsp flour

¼ tsp salt

¼ tsp turmeric

¼ tsp oregano

Directions

Preheat the oven to 350° F and grease a baking sheet with vegetable oil. Cut the peppers into wide, flat strips. Quickly run the pieces under cold water and shake off most of the moisture, but not all.

Pour the flour on a plate, and put the panko bread crumbs in a separate bowl. In a different bowl, whisk together the egg and the salt. Press each pepper piece into the flour, coating both sides with flour. Next, dip the peppers into the egg and salt mixture. Let the excess drip off, then place the peppers in the panko, coating both sides of the pepper. You can sprinkle the panko over the pepper pieces and gently press the coating in place as necessary to be sure each piece is well coated in breadcrumbs.

Place the peppers in a single layer on the baking sheet. Invite the energies of Jupiter to be prominent in the food. Bake for 15 minutes, then flip over and bake the pepper pieces for an additional 15 minutes or until crispy and golden brown.

To create the sauce, melt the butter over medium heat, then stir in the flour to create a thick roux. Warm the milk in a separate pot until it's steaming but not boiling, then add it to the flour and butter a little at a time. Stir the mixture constantly with a fork or whisk to get out any lumps. Once the mixture is a smooth texture, turn the heat off and add the turmeric, salt, and oregano. To serve, drizzle the sauce lightly over the peppers.

Saturn

Saturn is associated with death, the harvest, and the afterlife. Use Saturn-aligned ingredients to help facilitate spirit communication, bring freedom, dissolve unfortunate alliances or circumstances, encourage peace, or bring abundance.

Barley
Beets
Carrots
Figs
Garlic
Grains
Grapes
Mushrooms
Onions
Parsley
Parsnips
Potatoes

Rosemary
Sweet potatoes
Turnips
Wheat

ROASTED ROSEMARY TURNIPS

Effects: Eat to encourage peace and bring freedom from conflict.

Makes: 6 to 8 servings

Ingredients

4 turnips

½ C finely chopped walnuts

1 tbsp oil

¼ tsp salt

2 tsp rosemary

2 tbsp butter

Directions

Preheat the oven to 350° F. Wash and peel the turnips, then cut off the ends. Cut the turnips into bite-sized pieces. Put them in a baking dish along with the walnuts and toss with oil and salt. Add the rosemary and think of the energies of Saturn entering the food as you do so. Add the 2 tbsp of butter to the top of the turnips, separating it into small pieces. Bake for about 30 to 35 minutes or until turnips are tender.

SKULLS AND SICKLES COUSCOUS

Effects: Eat before communicating with spirits or leave as an offering to honor the dead.

Makes: 4 to 6 servings

Ingredients

1½ C vegetable broth

1⅓ C couscous

3 tbsp butter, divided

⅛–¼ tsp salt

8 oz. white button mushrooms

1 small onion

1 clove garlic

4 tbsp fresh parsley, plus more for garnish

Directions

Bring the vegetable broth and salt to a boil. Stir in the couscous and 1 tbsp butter. Let the mixture simmer for a minute or two, then turn off the heat and cover the pot. Let it sit covered for 5 to 10 minutes as you prepare the other ingredients. To create the mushroom skulls, first slice the mushrooms in half. Then use a chopstick or toothpick to carefully bore two wide, deep, eyehole-shaped indentations into the upper half of the mushroom cap. Next, use a paring knife to add a couple of small, slanted lines for the nasal cavities. Put a few vertical lines on the lower part of the mushroom cap to make the teeth of the skull. Think of your ancestors or other loved ones who have passed on

as you carve the mushrooms. Cut the onion in half, then slice it into thin half-circles to make the sickles. Mince the garlic and chop the parsley. Heat the remaining 2 tbsp butter in a pan over medium-high heat, then sauté the mushrooms, onion, parsley, and garlic for about 3 minutes or until the mushrooms are tender and the onions are translucent. Fluff the couscous with a fork, making sure to break up any clumps. Serve the sautéed vegetables over a bed of warm couscous. Garnish with additional parsley if desired.

Uranus

Associated with revolution, eccentricity, and transformation, Uranus attuned ingredients are powerful agents for bringing about major change. Eat Uranus-attuned ingredients to increase your confidence in doing things your own way, or to encourage individuality or spark a revolutionary, transformative change.

Anise

Boysenberries

Broccolini

Cinnamon

Clove

Cocoa

Coffee

Eggplant

Gala apples

Grapefruit

Honeycrisp apples

Hybrid fruits and
    vegetables

Ice

Ice cream

Pineapple

Pink Lady apples

Plumcots

Sesame

Star anise

Tangelos

General notes

_____

_____

_____

_____

_____

_____

_____

_____

_____

STAR ANISE AND CINNAMON
ICED COFFEE

Effects: Drink to encourage transformation and innovative thinking.

Makes: 1 serving

Ingredients

1 clove star anise

1 C ice

1 C brewed coffee, cold

1 tbsp sugar

⅛ tsp cinnamon

Directions

Crush the star anise with a mortar and pestle or meat tenderizer until it's powdered with no large, hard chunks. Add all the remaining ingredients to a blender or food processor and blend until frothy. Think of Uranus rotating on its near-sideways axis, different from the rotation of other planets.

ROASTED SESAME EGGPLANT

Effects: Eat to encourage change and share to bring
transformation and revolution.

Makes: 4 to 6 servings

Ingredients

2 medium eggplants

1 tsp salt

3 tbsp olive oil

1 tbsp sesame oil

2 garlic cloves, minced

1 tbsp toasted sesame
seeds

Directions

Cut the eggplant into large cubes, around 1½ inches in size.
Place in a bowl and sprinkle on the salt. Let the eggplant
sit with the salt on it for about an hour. Preheat the oven
to 400° F. Add the olive oil, sesame oil, and garlic. Toss
the eggplant to coat the pieces evenly. Invite the energies of the planet Uranus to enter the food.
Transfer the eggplant to an oven-safe
pan and bake for about 30 minutes or
until the eggplant is tender. Sprinkle
with sesame seeds and serve.

Neptune

Neptune is associated with dreams, inspiration, psychic abilities, enlightenment, fantasy, and compassion. Use Neptune-aligned foods to encourage good dreams or prophecy, to increase ESP and intuition, to bring about enlightenment, or to help soothe a volatile situation.

Cabbage

Cannabis

Celery

Cucumbers

Honeydew melons

Leeks

Lettuce

Nori

Poppy seeds

Radishes

Sea salt

Water chestnuts

Watercress

Wild leeks

General notes

_____

_____

_____

_____

PURPLE CABBAGE COLESLAW

Effects: Eat to boost psychic awareness or to bring prophetic dreams that reveal the hidden roots of a situation.

Makes: 4 to 6 servings

Ingredients

4 C red cabbage	1 C mayonnaise
2 large carrots	2 tsp sugar
1 stalk celery	⅛–¼ tsp salt
7 radishes	

Directions

Shred the cabbage, carrots, celery, and radishes using a box grater. Put the shredded vegetables in a large bowl, and stir in the mayonnaise, sugar, and salt. Start with just ⅛ tsp salt, mix thoroughly, and taste it. If it needs more salt, you can add up to another ⅛ tsp, but be sure to incorporate it in very tiny increments until you achieve the desired taste. It's easy to add too much salt and overpower the natural flavors of the vegetables. As you mix the ingredients, ask for the vibrations of the planet Neptune to enter the bowl. Serve this slaw as a side salad, or use it to top a veggie burger or fish filet.

NEPTUNE ROLL
. . . .

Effects: Eat to bring pleasant dreams and new inspiration.
Makes: 6 to 8 servings

Ingredients
For the rice

2 C short grain rice

3 tbsp rice vinegar

1 tbsp sugar

¼ tsp sea salt

For the rolls

1 cucumber

2 carrots

1 avocado

1 C water chestnuts,
    drained

1 can tuna or crab
    (optional)

Wasabi paste or soy
    sauce (optional)

4 sheets of dried nori
    for sushi

Directions
Rinse the rice multiple times, until the water is clear. Combine it with 2½ C water and bring to a boil. When it starts boiling, reduce the heat to low and cover the pot. Cook for about 13 to 15 minutes undisturbed until rice is tender and water is absorbed. Transfer the cooked rice to a large mixing bowl. Drizzle the rice vinegar and sprinkle the sugar and salt over the rice. Gently drag a thin wooden paddle or chopstick through the rice to encourage it to cool and

incorporate the vinegar, sugar, and salt evenly without breaking the delicate grains.

While the rice is cooling, peel the cucumber and carrots, and slice them into narrow strips. Remove the peel and pit from the avocado, then cut it into thin slices. Finely dice the water chestnuts. Drain the tuna or crab if you're using any. Once the rice reaches room temperature, put about ½ C rice in the center of each nori sheet. Make only one at a time. Push the rice down and spread it out on the wrapper in a big square, going nearly to the edges of the wrapper on each side. Then arrange about ¼ of the avocado, cucumber, and carrot slices in a horizontal line along the middle of the rice. Add a sprinkling of water chestnuts and the optional crab or tuna. Roll the bottom half of the nori wrapper over the filling away from you and gently pull it down and back toward you to make a tight roll. Continue rolling the sushi log away from you, then wet your fingertips to apply some water to the top edge of the sushi wrap so that it stays sealed. (If you've ever rolled a joint or a cigarette, you'll find the motions of rolling sushi second nature.) As you roll each sushi log, think of the power of Neptune. With a sharp knife, carefully cut each sushi roll into slices about 1 to 1½ inches thick.

For a faster, easier option, make a sushi bowl: Combine the rice and vegetables in a bowl along with the crab or tuna, and top it all with a sprinkling of crushed nori wrapper. Enjoy your sushi with wasabi or soy sauce if desired.

Pluto

Pluto is associated with the undercurrents of reality, the subconscious, and the underworld. It represents all that dwells deep within and on the flipside of what we see on the surface. Use Pluto-attuned recipes to bring transformation, spark renewal or regeneration, bring revolution, banish unwanted energies, reveal what is hidden, make the truth come to the surface, or encourage the healing of deep emotional wounds.

Anise	Honey
Barley	Licorice
Black beauty grapes	Mint
Blackberries	Mushrooms
Caraway	Parsnips
Cocoa	Plums
Coffee	Potatoes
Dark chocolate	Raisins
Eggplant	Rye
Grapes	Star anise

BROWN BUTTER PLUM AND RAISIN COOKIES

Effects: Enjoy to encourage transformation, self-love, and deep healing.

Makes: 6 to 8 servings

Ingredients

1½ C flour

½ tsp baking soda

¼ tsp salt

¼ tsp ground nutmeg

¾ C sugar

½ C milk

1 egg

½ tsp vanilla

¾ stick butter plus
  more for greasing

2 plums

1 C raisins

Directions

Preheat oven to 400° F. Mix together the flour, baking soda, salt, nutmeg, sugar, milk, egg, and vanilla. Heat the butter in a pan on the stove over medium-high heat for about five minutes, until the butter begins to brown. As the butter transforms, invite the energies of Pluto to enter the butter. Stir the brown butter into the cookie dough. Cut the plum into small pieces, then stir it into the dough along with the raisins. Scoop out tablespoon-sized balls of dough and place them about two or three inches apart on a greased cookie sheet. Gently pat them down to flatten but keep them at least ¼ inch thick at minimum. Bake for about 10 minutes or until the edges begin to look crisp.

DARK CHOCOLATE-DIPPED
BLACKBERRIES WITH MINT

Effects: Eat to banish unwanted energies.
Makes: 2 to 4 servings

Ingredients

1 C dark chocolate
  chips

2 C blackberries

¼ C fresh mint
  leaves

Melt the chocolate chips in a heavy saucepan over low heat, stirring slowly and frequently. Use a teaspoon to lower the blackberries into the melted chocolate and gently roll them around until they're nicely coated on all sides. Imagine the thorns of the blackberry bush repelling any unwanted energies in your life as you coat the berries in the chocolate. Place the blackberries on wax paper to cool. Serve a handful of the dark chocolate-dipped blackberries with a few fresh mint leaves for garnish.

General notes

General notes

Section 5

✦ · ✦ ☆ ✦ · ✦

Recipes for Magickal Goals

Look to this section for quick ingredient and recipe ideas arranged by their magickal effect.

Joy

Try these foods to encourage happiness and good cheer. These ingredients are also good for inviting friendship.

Apples

Bananas

Basil

Blueberries

Cherries

Chocolate

Dragon fruit

Grapes

Nuts

Oranges

Rosemary

Strawberries

Tomatoes

Vanilla

Watermelon

General notes

_____

_____

_____

_____

HAPPY MONKEY
CHOCOLATE BANANA BREAD

Effects: Eat to encourage good cheer.

Makes: 6 to 8 servings

Ingredients

1½ C flour	3 bananas
¾ tsp baking soda	½ C butter, melted
1 tsp baking powder	½ C milk
¼ tsp salt	2 tsp vanilla extract
1 C brown sugar	½ C chocolate chips

Directions

Preheat the oven to 350° F. Mix together the flour, baking soda, baking powder, and salt. In a separate bowl, mix together the brown sugar, banana, and melted butter. Use the back of a fork to mash the banana into the brown sugar, making sure there are no large chunks. Add the milk and vanilla extract to the banana and sugar mixture, then mix that all together with the bowl of dry ingredients. Finally, add the chocolate chips. Mix clockwise as you think of different things that make you feel happy. Imagine these feelings flowing into the batter, grinning as big as you can. If you like, imagine a playful monkey smiling at the bread with you. Bake the batter in a greased loaf pan for 45 to 60 minutes, or until the top is firm but springy to the touch.

JOYFUL DRAGON SMOOTHIE

Effects: Drink to encourage a positive attitude and increase feelings of happiness and joy.

Makes: 1 serving

Ingredients

1 C orange juice

½ C frozen dragon fruit

½ C ice

¼ tsp fresh basil

3 fresh or frozen strawberries

1 tsp honey or sugar (optional)

Directions

Add all ingredients to a blender and pulse in short bursts until smooth, smiling as the blender whirls. Envision yourself as a powerful dragon feeling extremely happy, smiling widely. Envision your powerful emotions flowing into the smoothie as you mix it.

CHEERING ROSEMARY BASIL BUTTER BAKE

Effects: Eat to bring comfort and improve a dismal mood.

Makes: 4 to 6 servings

Ingredients

½ C butter	3 yellow squash
3 tbsp fresh rosemary	2 C cherry tomatoes
3 tbsp fresh basil	½ tsp salt
3 zucchini	

Directions

Preheat oven to 350° F. Melt butter over low heat and add the chopped herbs. Heat until fragrant. Envision a happy scene as you smell the herbs. Next, slice the zucchini and squash into 1-inch-thick pieces, and place these in a deep baking dish. Add the tomatoes one by one as you think of something you like with each tomato. Sprinkle the whole dish with salt, and drizzle the rosemary-basil butter all over it. Roast in the oven for about 25–30 minutes until the squash is tender.

Protection

Use these ingredients to fortify defenses, bring protection, and increase strength and courage.

Beans

Black-eyed peas

Blackberries

Carrots

Cinnamon

Cumin

Eggs

Garlic

Kale

Mustard

Nuts

Okra

Onions

Oregano

Peanuts

Pepper

Spinach

General notes

_____

_____

_____

_____

_____

PEANUT GARLIC
PROTECTION NOODLES

Effects: Eat for protection, strength, and increased vitality.
Makes: 4 servings

Ingredients

8 oz. spaghetti or linguine

3 tbsp oil, divided

3 cloves garlic, minced

3 carrots, peeled and thinly sliced

1 onion, thinly sliced

1 bunch of kale, chopped

1¼ tbsp soy sauce, divided

2 tbsp peanut butter

1½ tsp garlic powder

¼ tsp powdered ginger

Directions

Begin by prepping the vegetables and bringing a large pot of salted water to a boil. Once the water comes to a boil, add the noodles and cook until al dente. Heat 1 tbsp of the oil and the minced garlic in a pan over medium-high heat. Add the carrots and cook for two minutes. Add the onion and cook for two more minutes or until carrots look vibrant and tender, then add the kale and 1 tbsp soy sauce and cook for one minute. Drain the noodles. Heat the remaining 2 tbsp of oil in a large pot or pan. Once the oil is hot, add the noodles and toss to coat. Add the remaining soy sauce and the peanut butter. Stir and scatter the noodles with a fork to heat and distribute the peanut butter. Think of any threats or dangers being flung far away. Sprinkle on the garlic powder as you imagine an impenetrable wall of protection surrounding yourself and your loved ones. Add the vegetables and toss before serving.

General notes

_____

_____

_____

_____

_____

_____

_____

_____

_____

_____

_____

_____

_____

_____

_____

_____

_____

BLACKBERRY BARRIER COBBLER

Effects: Eat for protection against enemies and to increase strength and tenacity.

Makes: 4 servings

Ingredients

1 stick of butter

1 C flour

1 tsp baking powder

1 C sugar

1 C milk

⅛–¼ tsp cinnamon

2 C blackberries

Directions

Preheat the oven to 350° F. Place the stick of butter in a baking pan and heat until the butter melts. Mix together the flour, baking powder, and sugar, then add the milk and the cinnamon. For just a light hint of cinnamon flavor, use only ⅛ tsp cinnamon powder (for a stronger cinnamon taste, increase the amount to ¼ tsp). Pour the batter over the melted butter. There is no need to stir the butter into the batter. Arrange the blackberries on top of the batter so that the berries are equally distributed. As you place the berries, think of the protective thorns of the blackberry bush and envision a thick wall of blackberries surrounding yourself, your home, or whatever else you are wanting to strengthen and protect. Bake for 35–40 minutes or until the top is golden.

SPICY SPANISH RICE

Effects: Eat to strengthen defenses and increase courage.

Makes: 4 servings

Ingredients

1½ C rice

1 15-oz. can stewed tomatoes and green chilies, drained

1 onion (medium yellow or white)

1 green or red bell pepper

2 tbsp oil or butter

¾ tsp chili powder

1 tsp garlic powder

¼ tsp black pepper

½ tsp cumin

½ tsp salt

½ tsp paprika

Directions

Cook rice according to your favorite method. One way is to add the rice to a pot with 3 C water. Bring to a boil, then reduce heat to low, cover, and let it cook undisturbed for fifteen minutes. Dice the bell pepper and onion, then sauté in 2 tbsp oil or butter over medium high heat for about five minutes, until vegetables are vibrant and fragrant. Add the bell pepper and onion to the cooked rice along with the remaining ingredients. For a spicier or milder rice, add or subtract ¼ tsp chili powder from the recipe. Mix the spices into the rice by dragging a chopstick or wooden paddle through it swiftly but gently. The goal is to avoid crushing the grains of rice. Imagine yourself as a strong, impassioned, and ferocious beast as you stir the rice, and envision this wild power going into the food.

Purification

Just as physical dirt sticks to our skin, metaphysical "dirt" can stick to our auras. Use these ingredients to refresh your energies when you're feeling like a general or specific "ickiness" is clinging to you or weighing you down.

Bay	Lime
Beans	Mint
Black pepper	Parsley
Black-eyed peas	Pickles
Chili powder	Red pepper flakes
Chilies	Rosemary
Cucumbers	Sage
Dill	Salt
Garlic	Thyme
Jalapeños	Vinegar
Lavender	Water
Lemons	Watermelon

PURIFYING WATERMELON FREEZE

Effects: Drink to refresh and purify your energies.
Makes: 1 serving

Ingredients

2 C watermelon cut
   into 1-inch chunks

1 radish

1 tbsp honey

¾ C water

2 tsp lime or lemon
   juice

Directions

Place the watermelon chunks in the freezer until frozen. Trim the ends off the radish. Place the radish and frozen watermelon in a blender or food processor. Add the honey, water, and the lime or lemon juice. Blend until pureed. As the mixture blends, imagine any stale energies or negative vibes you'd like to banish being driven away by the aggressive action of the blender. Pour the mixture into a drinking glass, then gently stir the beverage as you imagine a fresh flow of positive energy coming to you.

REFRESHING CUCUMBER SALAD

Effects: Eat to feel refreshed and to welcome change.

Makes: 4 to 6 servings

Ingredients

4 cucumbers

1 C cherry tomatoes

⅓ C plain yogurt

1 tbsp dill weed

¼ tsp pepper

½ tsp salt

Directions

Peel the cucumber and chop into cubes. Cut the cherry tomatoes into halves if desired, or leave them whole. Place the cucumbers in a large bowl along with the yogurt, dill, pepper, and salt. Mix gently until well-combined, imagining a gentle and refreshing breeze sweeping through the bowl as you do so. Finally, add the tomatoes to complete the salad.

General notes

CHECKERBOARD BEANS

Effects: Eat to banish unwanted influences, restore balance, and reset your energies.

Makes: 6 to 8 servings

Ingredients

2 cans black beans (or 3¼ C prepared dried beans)

2 cans black-eyed peas (or 3¼ C prepared dried black-eyed peas)

¼–½ tsp salt

½–1½ tsp red pepper flakes

¼ tsp black or white pepper

Directions

Drain and rinse the black beans until the water runs nearly clear. Don't drain the black-eyed peas. In a large pot, mix the black beans, black-eyed peas, salt, black pepper, and red pepper flakes. One teaspoon of the red pepper flakes delivers a mild yet palpable heat. If you want only a hint of spice, use only ½ tsp of red pepper flakes. If you want it extra spicy, go for more than a teaspoon. Heat on medium and stir occasionally, alternating between clockwise and counterclockwise motions. As you stir counterclockwise, think of something you wish to let go of or lessen, such as worry or toxic patterns. As you stir clockwise, think of something you wish to bring in or increase, such as more confidence, or focus and determination. The beans are ready once they're heated throughout. Serve with cornbread or rice, or enjoy as a hearty side dish.

Success

Success is a very versatile magickal goal that applies to a multitude of situations. Whether you're hoping for success in landing a job or wishing for a successful night out with your crew, a spell for success can help. Ingredients useful in magick for success include a wide variety of foods with solar associations as well as foods believed to boost confidence or attract general good fortune and luck. Success-bringing foods include:

Apples	Oranges
Basil	Oregano
Bay	Rhubarb
Beans	Rosemary
Cinnamon	Squash
Corn	Vanilla
Ginger	

ORANGE SUPREME PARFAIT

· ·

Effects: Eat to bring success.
Makes: 2 servings

Ingredients

2 oranges   1 tsp cinnamon

4 C whipped cream

Directions

Cut the ends off the oranges and stand them up with one
of the cut sides facing down against the cutting board.
Use a paring knife to supreme the oranges: carefully carve
around the inside rim of the orange peel to separate the
flesh of the orange from the rind and pith. Next, make a
cut along each side of the membranes dividing the orange
segments. You'll be left with some very juicy, membrane-
free orange segments. Once you've supremed both oranges,
mix the cinnamon into the whipped cream, stirring as
gently as possible. Layer the whipped cream and orange
supreme into two clear glasses, making at least two layers
of whipped cream and two layers of orange supreme in
each glass. As you create each layer, make another wish for
success.

SQUASH WHEELS OF FORTUNE

Effects: Eat to energize your goals and invite success.
Makes: 4 servings

Ingredients

2 yellow squash

1 tbsp olive oil

⅛ tsp salt

½ tsp oregano

½ C shredded parmesan

Directions

Preheat the oven to 350° F. Slice the yellow squash into ¼-inch-thick discs. Arrange the slices in a single layer on a baking sheet and think about the foundation you have laid for success as you do so. Brush the tops of the squash with olive oil as you think of how you will nourish your dreams, then sprinkle on the salt and oregano as you wish for luck and opportunity to find you. Top each squash slice with a pinch of shredded parmesan. As you add the parmesan, imagine the experiences and emotions of being wildly successful. See yourself achieving your goal. Bake the squash wheels for about 10 to 13 minutes, then broil for another two to three minutes until the cheese is bubbling and begins to turn a light golden brown in some places. As you eat each piece, think to yourself, "I am successful!"

SWEET CORN CASSEROLE

· ·

Effects: Eat to bring success, good luck, and opportunity.
Makes: 4 to 6 servings

Ingredients

2 15-oz. cans whole
  kernel corn

½ C milk

2 tbsp flour

⅛ tsp pepper

¼ tsp salt

1 tsp basil

3 eggs

¼ C shredded
  parmesan (optional)

¼ C shredded cheddar
  (optional)

1–2 tbsp honey
  (optional)

Directions

Preheat the oven to 350° F. Drain the corn, then pour
it in a large bowl. Add all the other ingredients, and stir
clockwise in a spiral motion working from the outside
toward the center. As you combine the ingredients, envision the success you desire. Picture it vividly and imagine
the emotions the success will bring. Pour the mixture into
a buttered or oiled baking dish and bake for about 40–45
minutes or until set. Lightly drizzle honey over the top of
the casserole if desired.

Love

Use these ingredients to open opportunities for new romance or to strengthen feelings of love, passion, and enchantment. These foods are also good for encouraging compassion, grace, nurturing, and healing, or for boosting abundance and enhancing beauty and glamor.

Apples
Apricots
Avocados
Bananas
Basil
Cherries
Chocolate
Cinnamon
Cocoa
Dragon fruit
Ginger
Grapes
Honey

Olive oil
Olives
Peaches
Pomegranate
Rosemary
Strawberries
Thyme
Tomatoes
Vanilla

DRAGON FRUIT CHEESECAKE

Effects: Eat to encourage feelings of love and passion.
Makes: 6 to 8 servings

Ingredients

2 8-oz. packages cream
cheese

1 C plus one 1 tbsp
sugar

2 tbsp water

1 C frozen dragon fruit
pieces

1 tsp vanilla extract

2 eggs

½ C sour cream

2 C dark chocolate or
semi-sweet choco-
late chips

1 graham cracker pie
crust

Directions

Set the cream cheese out to soften for about 30 to 45 minutes. Preheat the oven to 400° F. Place the dragon fruit in
a blender or food processor along with 2 tbsp water and
1 tbsp of the sugar. Blend until pureed, then heat this in
a saucepan on the stovetop over medium high heat for
about 7 minutes, stirring frequently. Turn off the heat and
let the sauce cool as you mix the cheesecake. Put the cream
cheese in a large mixing bowl, and pour in the remaining cup of sugar. Using the back of a fork, mash the sugar
into the cream cheese, slowly dragging the fork through
the mixture while pushing down. Add the vanilla extract

and eggs, then add the sour cream. Stir until everything is thoroughly combined.

Pour the cheesecake mixture into the graham cracker pie crust, leaving about ⅛–¼ inch of room at the top. Once the dragon fruit sauce has cooled to the touch, drizzle 2 tbsp of it on to the top of the cheesecake. Using a chopstick or the tip of a butter knife, slowly and carefully swirl the sauce in spiral patterns over the cake. Think of love and passion as you swirl in the sauce. In several places, gently push the chopstick or butter knife deeper into the cheesecake batter so that the sauce seeps throughout the batter. Reserve the remaining dragon fruit sauce. Bake the cheesecake in the oven for about 15 minutes, then reduce to 350° F and bake for an additional 30 to 45 minutes until the cheesecake is set.

On the stovetop over medium low heat, melt the chocolate chips. Stir constantly, and remove the pan from the heat every 30 seconds or so to let it cool a bit as you continue to stir. It should only take a couple minutes to melt the chocolate chips. Let the chocolate cool a little, then spoon it onto the top of the cheesecake. Use the back of a spoon to gently spread the chocolate out in a layer covering the top of the cheesecake. Next, spoon on the remaining dragon fruit sauce, swirling it through the chocolate with a chopstick or tip of a butter knife. Continue to cool the cheesecake, first on the countertop until no longer hot, then in the refrigerator for 1 to 2 hours.

ROSEMARY TOMATO BRUSCHETTA

Effects: Eat to invite love, or share with a loved one to bring out feelings of affection and encourage romantic declarations.

Makes: 6 to 8 servings

Ingredients

1 loaf french bread

¼ C olive oil

2 cloves garlic

2 tbsp fresh basil

4 Roma tomatoes

2 tbsp fresh rosemary

1 C shredded mozzarella

Directions

Cut the bread loaf in half lengthwise, then drizzle or brush with olive oil. Mince the garlic, chop the basil, take the rosemary leaves off the stems, and dice the tomatoes. Scatter the minced garlic over the bread, then place the bread in the oven on broil just until the bread begins to toast. Remove the bread from the oven, and top it with the tomatoes, rosemary, and basil. Fill your heart with a feeling of love, and direct this energy onto the topped bread. Broil the bread in the oven for one minute. Then take it out of the oven again and sprinkle on the mozzarella. Broil for an additional minute or two until the cheese is thoroughly melted. It will cook quickly, so stay near the oven.

APPLE LOVE MUFFINS

Effects: Eat to invite and welcome more love and passion.

Makes: 6 to 12 servings

Ingredients

2 apples	2 tsp cinnamon
2 C flour	1 tsp allspice
2½ tsp baking powder	1 egg
½ C brown sugar	1¼ C milk
1 C white sugar	

For topping

⅛ C butter	⅛ C flour
¼ C brown sugar	1 tsp cinnamon

Directions

Preheat the oven to 350° F. Peel and dice the apples. In a large bowl, mix together the flour, baking powder, ½ C brown sugar, and 1 C white sugar. Add 2 tsp cinnamon and 1 tsp allspice as you imagine yourself filled with passion and ardor. Add the egg and milk, then finally stir in the apple. Think of something you love as you add the apples and let this feeling flow into the bowl. Stir clockwise, then do the final few stirs in a heart shape. Spoon the batter into a greased muffin tin, filling the cups about

⅔ full. In a small bowl, mash together the butter, ¼ C brown sugar, ⅛ C flour, and 1 tsp cinnamon to create a crumble. Top the muffin cups with a sprinkling of the crumble, then bake for about 25 minutes until the tops are firm and springy.

Peace

Use these ingredients to bring peace, strengthen friendships, encourage cooperation and compassion, soothe anxiety, and calm volatile situations.

Almonds	Lavender
Apples	Mango
Apricots	Marjoram
Avocados	Mint
Bananas	Olive oil
Basil	Olives
Beans	Papaya
Cherries	Parsley
Chickpeas	Peaches
Coconut	Pears
Grapes	Peas

Rosemary

Sage

Soybeans

Strawberries

Sunflower seeds

Thyme

Tomato

Vanilla

Watermelon

White beans

General notes

_____

_____

_____

_____

_____

_____

_____

_____

_____

_____

_____

_____

_____

_____

_____

_____

_____

PEACE PIZZA

· · · · · · · · · · · · · · · · · · · ·

Effects: Eat to bring peace and reconcili-
ation, or to foster peaceful and pleasant
cooperation.

Makes: 4 to 6 servings

Ingredients

For dough

2½ tsp yeast	½ tsp salt
1½ tsp sugar	1 tsp marjoram
¾ C warm water	2 tbsp oil
2⅓ C flour	

For sauce

6 large tomatoes, or 12 roma tomatoes	1 tbsp fresh thyme
3 tbsp butter	1–2 tbsp fresh rosemary
1 clove garlic	Salt to taste
½–¾ C water	

For toppings

1 small can sliced black olives	8 oz. shredded mozzarella
1 tbsp fresh basil	⅛–¼ C parmesan (optional)

Directions

Mix together the yeast, sugar, and warm water. Make sure the water is very warm but not so hot that it's uncomfortable to touch. You can use a thermometer for accuracy; the water should be around 110 degrees Fahrenheit. Below 105° F might not be warm enough to activate the yeast, while any temperature above 130° F will kill it. Set this yeast mixture to the side. In a large bowl, mix the flour, salt, and marjoram. Wait about 5–15 minutes for the yeast to activate. Once the yeast mixture looks bubbly and its volume has visibly increased, add it to the dry ingredients. If the yeast mixture isn't bubbly, try again— the yeast might be old, or the water may have been the wrong temperature. Next, add the olive oil, then mix the ingredients until it comes together into a ball. You can add a little more water if needed. Knead the dough until it feels cohesive and stretchy. Dust the dough ball with flour and place it in a lightly oiled bowl or pot that you can cover. Keep the dough in the tightly covered container for about an hour to two hours, until it has doubled in size.

As you wait for the dough to rise, you can start on the sauce. Put a pot of water on to boil, and score an "x" shaped cut into the bottom of each tomato. Place the tomatoes in the boiling water for just a minute or two, then put them into a bowl of cold water to stop the cooking. Remove the peels, then cut the tomatoes into small pieces. In a saucepan, heat 3 tbsp butter over medium heat until melted. Add the minced garlic and stir until it becomes fragrant. Add the tomatoes and ½ to ¾ C of water, and turn the heat down to low. Add the thyme and rosemary, and add a small sprinkle of salt if desired. Think of all the ingredients coming together in harmony and the warring factions to whom you wish to bring peace also coming together in a peaceful way. Let the tomatoes simmer on low heat for about ten minutes, then turn off the heat and cover the pot. While the sauce is resting, slice the olives into thin circular slices, and gently remove the basil leaves from the stem.

Once the dough has risen, divide it into fourths to make four personal pizzas, or into halves to create two larger pizzas. Place each dough portion on a floured surface and use a floured rolling pin to roll it out to about ⅛ inch thick. Preheat the oven to 400° F. Place the pizza dough on a greased pizza pan or cookie sheet, reshaping as necessary once the dough is on the oiled pan. If you like, you can make the dough into a heart shape to call more love into the recipe. Roll up the edges on the outer perimeter of the dough to create a doughier crust. Top each pizza with the tomato mixture, then add a layer of shredded mozzarella cheese. Finish it with olives and fresh basil leaves as well as a light sprinkling of parmesan if desired. Bake for about 20 to 30 minutes or until dough is cooked throughout and cheese is melted. Cooking time will vary depending on the thickness of the dough and the size of the pizzas.

General notes

_____

_____

_____

_____

_____

_____

_____

_____

_____

_____

_____

_____

_____

SMOOTH IT OVER SMOOTHIE

Effects: Share to reconcile differences or to forge peaceful, positive alliances.

Makes: 2 servings

Ingredients

2 C strawberries

2 bananas

2 C almond milk

Fresh mint leaves (optional)

Directions

Cut the ends off the strawberries to remove the leaves. Peel the bananas and break them into large chunks. Place the fruit and almond milk in a blender or food processor, and blend until it reaches the desired consistency. As the mixture blends, think of conflicts and contention being processed and transformed into a new understanding. Serve this drink with fresh mint if desired.

HARMONIOUS MINI CHIMICHANGAS

Effects: Share to encourage peace.

Makes: 4 servings

Ingredients

2 C refried beans	½ tsp salt
½ tsp thyme	Vegetable oil
2 avocados	8 flour tortillas
6–8 roma tomatoes	

Directions

Heat the refried beans over medium heat until warm. Dice the tomatoes and slice the avocados into ¼-inch thick slices. Then place ¼ C of beans in the center of each tortilla. Flatten down the beans into a thin layer, ¼–½ inches thick. Top the beans with 2 tbsp of diced tomatoes, and sprinkle on a small pinch of thyme. Speak your wishes for peace over each topped tortilla. Envision harmony and happiness. Fold in the sides of the tortilla, then fold the bottom and top of the tortilla inward to overlap in the middle, creating a sort of rectangular pouch or flattened burrito. The sides will want to come open but don't worry; they'll stay closed and seal up during the cooking process. Heat about ¼ inch of oil in a deep pan over medium-high to high heat. Place each mini chimichanga into the oil, seam side down. Let it cook for 20 to 30 seconds on each side. Top with slices of avocado and an additional tbsp of diced tomatoes for garnish. Sprinkle the avocado and tomato garnish with a small pinch of salt.

Prosperity

The key to increasing prosperity is gratitude, which requires being aware of your blessings. The more conscious you are of your current treasures, the greater ability you will have to generate more abundance in your life. Use these ingredients to help increase the flow of wealth heading your way.

Allspice

Basil

Bay

Beans

Cabbage

Cinnamon

Clove

Collard greens

Grains

Grapes

Kale

Maple syrup

Nutmeg

Olives

Oranges

Oregano

Pecans

Rice

Sesame

Spinach

Walnuts

General notes

ABUNDANCE SOUP

Effects: Eat to invite more abundance and prosperity into your life.

Makes: 4 to 6 servings

Ingredients

6 C water

Any fresh or canned vegetables

1½ tsp salt

⅛–¼ tsp pepper

1½ tsp oregano

2 tsp garlic powder

1 can stewed tomatoes

Directions

This recipe is very versatile and can be made with any beans or vegetables you have on hand. Green beans, pinto beans, corn, kale, spinach–any of these work great if you happen to have them on hand. Mix all ingredients in a large pot. Think of the journey that each ingredient made to get to you as you add it to the soup. Let a feeling of gratitude flow from your heart into the soup. Then, envision that you are drawing in resources as you stir clockwise. Trace a pentacle shape and/or a dollar sign with the spoon every so often. Heat until all the vegetables are tender and the broth has become flavorful. Boiled noodles and chicken can be added if desired. If using chicken, cut into small bite-sized pieces and add to the soup at the beginning of the cooking process. Any chicken added to the soup must be cooked all the way through.

PROSPERITY POTATO BITES

Effects: Eat to invite prosperity.

Makes: 4 servings

Ingredients

2 medium potatoes, peeled

¼–⅓ C milk

½ tsp salt

½ small onion

1 C fresh spinach

1 tbsp butter

1 egg

1 tsp oregano

½ C flour

¼ C panko breadcrumbs

½ C shredded parmesan (optional)

Vegetable oil

Directions

Cut the potatoes into large chunks. Place them in a pot and cover with cold water by about an inch. Boil the potatoes until tender. Drain the water, then mash the potatoes using a potato masher or the bottom of a sturdy, heatproof, flat-bottomed cup or small bowl. Add the milk and salt to the potatoes to create a very stiff mashed potato consistency. You only need to add enough milk to make the mixture a little easier to stir. Dice the onion and chop the spinach. Sauté the onion in 1 tbsp butter. Add the onions to the potatoes, then mix in the egg. Finally, stir in the spinach and oregano, envisioning a great flow of wealth coming to you as you blend the mixture. Use a large spoon or ice cream scoop to scoop out dollops of the potato mix, one at a time. Shape each dollop into a flattened ball or oval shape.

Pour the flour and breadcrumbs into a shallow dish, then toss the flattened potato bites in the mixture, ensuring both sides are coated. Fry in small batches in hot oil for about two minutes per side or until golden brown. Place on a wire rack to drain and sprinkle with salt immediately, while still hot.

General notes

_____

_____

_____

_____

_____

_____

_____

_____

_____

_____

CINNAMON ORANGE CAKE

Effects: Eat to illuminate your blessings and invite
increasing prosperity.

Makes: 6 to 8 servings

Ingredients

1 C flour	½ C butter
1 C semolina flour	1 C sugar
1 tbsp baking powder	1 C milk
1 tbsp cinnamon	1 lemon
½ tsp salt	3 eggs

For syrup

1½ C water	¼–½ C walnut halves
1½ C sugar	(optional)
Peel of 1 orange	

Directions

Preheat oven to 350° F. Mix together both types of flour,
baking powder, cinnamon, and salt. In a separate bowl,
mash the butter into 1 C sugar, then stir in the eggs. Add
this to the dry ingredients, then mix in 1 C milk. Zest the
whole lemon, then cut the lemon in half. Add to the cake
batter the zest from the entire lemon and the juice from
only half of the lemon. Reserve the remaining half lemon;
you'll need it for the citrus syrup. Pour the batter into a

greased cake pan and bake for about 30 to 35 minutes. While the cake is cooling, start your orange sauce. Heat 1½ C water and 1½ C sugar in a saucepan over medium heat. Once the sugar dissolves, add the peel of one orange, and turn the heat to medium-low. Let the mixture simmer for about 7 to 8 minutes, then remove from heat. Remove the orange peel, and add the juice from the other half of the lemon. Stir to combine. Put the cake on a large plate, then slowly pour the warm syrup all over the top, letting the excess drip down the sides. Envision a flow of wealth and other blessings flowing your way as you pour the syrup. The syrup will be very thin, so pour slowly so the cake can absorb the liquid. If desired, arrange the walnut halves on top of the cake in the shape of a pentacle, spiral, dollar sign, or any other pattern.

Psychic Power

Use these ingredients to encourage intuition and improve psychic awareness. Enjoy before magick or divination, or anytime you want to heighten your awareness of psychic forces.

Anise

Apples

Bay

Cannabis

Caraway

Cinnamon

Clove

Coffee

Marjoram

Nutmeg

Pomegranate

Poppy seeds

Star anise

Thyme

Vanilla

General notes

_____

_____

_____

_____

_____

_____

_____

_____

_____

_____

_____

_____

_____

CINNAMON VANILLA CHEESECAKE
. . . .

Effects: Eat to open your psychic faculties.
Makes: 6 to 8 servings

Ingredients

2 8-oz. packages cream
   cheese

1 C sugar

2 eggs

1 tsp cinnamon powder

1 tsp vanilla extract

1 graham cracker pie
   crust

Directions

Set the cream cheese out for about half an hour until it softens. Preheat the oven to 400° F. Once the cream cheese is softened, put it in a large bowl. Add the sugar and mash the mixture together with the back of a fork until the sugar is thoroughly incorporated. Add the eggs, then stir in the cinnamon and vanilla as you imagine their powerful energies fusing with the mixture. As you continue to stir, spiraling outward from the center in a clockwise direction, imagine yourself being able to see what might be going on in the rest of the building you're in, then what might be going on in your neighborhood, your city, country, and your world. Fill the pie crust with the cream cheese mixture to about ¼ inch below the rim. Bake for 15 minutes, then reduce the heat to 350 and bake for 30 to 45 more minutes until set. Cool thoroughly, first on the countertop until nearly room temperature, then in the refrigerator for 1 to 2 hours.

General notes

_____

_____

_____

_____

_____

_____

_____

_____

_____

_____

_____

_____

_____

_____

_____

_____

_____

_____

_____

POMEGRANATE APPLE SPRITZER

• •

Effects: Drink before or during psychic readings to give your intuitive faculties extra support.

Makes: 1 serving

Ingredients

¼ C pomegranate juice

½ C apple juice

1 C club soda

¼-½ tsp vanilla extract

Directions

Combine the pomegranate juice and apple juice, then top with club soda. Add the vanilla extract and stir briskly for thirteen rotations. Finally, tap the cup three times with the spoon.

General notes

_____

_____

_____

_____

_____

_____

_____

_____

SPICED BUTTER COOKIES

Effects: Eat before magick or divination, or before bedtime to inspire prophetic dreams.

Makes: 6 to 8 servings

Ingredients

1 tsp coffee beans	¼ tsp salt
3 cloves star anise	1 C sugar
1¼ C flour	1 stick butter
½ tsp baking powder	2 eggs
½ tsp baking soda	1 tsp cinnamon
1 tsp nutmeg	

Directions

Set the butter out to soften about 30 minutes before you plan to begin making the cookies. Preheat the oven to 350° F. Grind the coffee beans in a coffee grinder and smash the star anise with a mortar and pestle or meat tenderizer until it's finely ground with no hard pieces. Mix together the flour, baking powder, baking soda, nutmeg, salt, star anise, coffee, and cinnamon. In a separate bowl, combine the butter with the sugar, then mix in the eggs. Combine this with the dry ingredients, and stir then

knead it gently to form a ball. It's easiest to use your clean hands. Be gentle and don't compress the dough too much; knead just enough until it stays together and is thoroughly blended. Make 1-inch balls of dough and place them at least two inches apart on a greased cookie sheet. Flatten each cookie slightly with your fingertips as you think, "May impressions be strong!" Then use the curved tip of a wet tablespoon to press a crescent moon shaped indentation into each cookie. Invite the power of the moon into the dough as you make each lunar glyph. The impressions will bake out, but the energy will remain. Bake the cookies for 8 to 10 minutes until the edges just begin to turn a dark golden brown and the tops of the cookies appear done and not doughy.

Health and Rejuvenation

Use these ingredients to help restore and encourage good health; fortify defenses; and boost vitality, strength, and stamina.

Apples	Blueberries
Avocados	Broccoli
Basil	Carrots
Beets	Cherries
Blackberries	Chili powder

Chocolate

Cilantro

Cranberries

Cumin

Eggs

Garlic

Ginger

Grapefruit

Grapes

Green beans

Honey

Kale

Lemons

Limes

Mint

Mushrooms

Mustard

Nuts

Olives

Onions

Oranges

Pepper

Peppers

Pumpkins

Rosemary

Sage

Squash

Tomatoes

Zucchini

SAUTÉED VEGGIE WRAPS

Effects: Eat to help maintain health or support healing.
Makes: 4 servings

Ingredients

1 zucchini

1 yellow squash

1 red bell pepper

1 clove garlic

1 tbsp olive oil

¼ tsp salt

4 spinach tortilla wraps

4 tbsp chopped cilantro
(optional)

For the spread

2 tbsp mayonnaise

1 tbsp yellow mustard

1 tbsp honey

½–¾ tsp black pepper

Directions

Cut the zucchini and squash into bite-size chunks and cut the bell pepper into thin strips. Mince the garlic. Heat the olive oil in a large pan and add the garlic and the bell peppers. Stir to coat the peppers in the oil. Let this cook for a full minute, then add the squash and zucchini. Stir the vegetables to distribute the oil, and add the salt. Sauté for three to five minutes until the vegetables are vibrant and tender yet still slightly crispy. Think of the health-supporting properties of the ingredients as they cook. If the vegetables are overcooked, they will lose a lot of flavor and nutrients, so stop cooking just as the veggies turn vibrant and become tender enough for your liking. Add the optional cilantro if desired once you reach the last 30 seconds of cooking time.

In a small bowl, mix the mayonnaise, mustard, honey, and black pepper to make a sauce. Put the cooked vegetables in the center of each wrap and top with the spread. Wrap it up like a burrito as you imagine perfect health, strength, and vitality. Also great as a taco filing or on a toasted sandwich roll.

General notes

_____

_____

_____

_____

_____

_____

_____

_____

_____

_____

_____

MARVELOUS
MUSHROOM TACOS

Effects: Eat to support healing, increase vitality, and boost energy.

Makes: 4 to 6 servings

Ingredients

For the filling

8 oz. white button mushrooms

1 small onion, diced

2 tbsp butter

1 tsp garlic powder

½ tsp chili powder

⅛ tsp salt

¼ tsp pepper

For the tortillas

Cooking oil

12 corn tortillas

For serving

1 avocado, pitted and sliced

1 small tomato, diced

1 handful cilantro, chopped

1 C shredded cheese

1 lime, cut into wedges

Directions

Cut the mushrooms into quarters. Heat the butter in a pan over medium-high heat, then sauté the mushrooms and onions until tender, seasoning with the garlic powder, chili powder, salt, and pepper. As you add the spices, focus on your will to have any illness driven out and away. Imagine an energy of vitality coursing through the food.

In a separate pan, heat the oil, then fry the tortillas one at a time for about 15 seconds on each side. Use a set of kitchen tongs to flip the tortilla and take it out of the oil when it's ready. Stand the tortillas vertically in a small bowl or place on a wire rack to drain. Place about ¼ C filling down the middle of each tortilla, topping with avocado, cilantro, tomato, cheese, and any other desired topping. Serve with lime wedges and squeeze a little lime juice on each taco if desired. Fold in half and enjoy.

General notes

_____

_____

_____

_____

_____

_____

_____

_____

_____

LIVELY STIR FRY

· ·

Effects: Eat to increase strength and energy, encourage healing, and support good health.

Makes: 4 to 6 servings

Ingredients

1 crown broccoli

3 carrots, peeled

1 bunch kale

3 cloves garlic

1 small red onion

2 tsp grated ginger (1 tsp powdered)

2 tbsp oil

3 tbsp soy sauce

Directions

Begin by preparing the vegetables. Imagine that you're cutting through any obstacles to good health as you slice and tear the vegetables, envisioning any baneful energies being ripped apart and dissipated. Chop the broccoli into bite-sized or smaller pieces, then slice the carrots into thin disks. Tear the kale into large pieces, about twice the size of bite-sized, as it will shrink as it cooks. Mince the garlic and slice the red onion into very thin slices. Heat the oil stovetop over high heat, in a wok or a large, deep pan. Once the oil is hot, add the broccoli, carrots, garlic, and ginger. Quickly stir to coat everything with oil. After about two minutes, add the kale, soy sauce, and red onion. Stir frequently as the vegetables cook. Think of the energy packed into each piece of vegetable, imagining the plants growing from the earth and eventually making their way into your pan. Once the broccoli becomes a more vibrant green and is slightly tender, the stir-fry is ready. Serve on its own as a side dish, or add to rice for a main course.

Calming

Use these ingredients to encourage calm, soothe volatile emotions, and bring balance and stability to a chaotic situation. These foods are also good for encouraging cooperation and compassion, and for easing anxiety and grief.

Almonds

Bananas

Cabbage

Chamomile

Coconut

Cucumbers

Dairy and non-dairy
    milk products

Lavender

Lettuce

Mango

Olive oil

Olives

Papaya

Pears

Potatoes

Sage

Vanilla

Watermelon

CALMING PEAR CRUMBLE

Effects: Eat to bring a calming, soothing energy.
Makes: 4 to 6 servings

Ingredients

6 fresh pears or 2 14.5–
oz. cans sliced pears

2 tsp vanilla extract

1 C flour

¼ C sugar

⅔ C brown sugar

1 stick of butter

Directions

Preheat the oven to 350° F. Peel and slice the pears into wedges if using fresh fruit. If you're using canned pears, drain them. Put the pears in a baking pan. Drizzle in the vanilla extract, then stir to distribute. Breathe deeply and think of a calming scene as you combine the pears with the vanilla. Envision a calming, lavender-hued light emanating from the fruit. Next, mix together the flour and sugars in a bowl. Cut in the butter, mashing it into the flour and sugar blend with a pastry blender or the back of a fork until you have a crumbly mixture with the texture of wet sand. Sprinkle the crumble mixture over the pears. Bake at 350 degrees for about 55 minutes to 1 hour, or until the crumble has browned.

MIDNIGHT SUNDAE

Effects: Eat to aid relaxation and encourage restful sleep.

Makes: 1 serving

Ingredients

½ C whipped cream

1 banana

1 tbsp chopped or slivered almonds

1 tbsp shredded coconut

3 cherries

Directions

Place the whipped cream in the center of a plate or bowl. Cut the banana into 1-inch-thick chunks. Arrange the banana pieces in a circle surrounding the whipped cream. Sprinkle the almonds on the whipped cream, and arrange the cherries. Top the whipped cream with the shredded coconut, thinking of what you wish to dream about as you add it. Conjure in your mind the most pleasant dream imaginable.

General notes

_____

_____

_____

_____

ROASTED LAVENDER AND
SAGE POTATOES

Effects: Eat these potatoes to help promote feelings of
calm.

Makes: 6 to 8 servings

Ingredients

2 lbs. potatoes (any
white or gold
variety)

3 tbsp olive oil

1 tsp salt

1 tsp ground sage

2½ tbsp lavender
flowers

½ C sour cream
(optional)

Directions

Preheat the oven to 350° F. Cut the potatoes into 1-inch
pieces, then put in a deep baking pan. Add the olive oil
and toss the potatoes to coat them with the oil. Add the
salt and sage one at a time, gently tossing the potatoes
between each round so that the herbs and salt are equally
distributed. Imagine a calm and peaceful natural scene as
you toss the potatoes in the seasonings. Bake for about
45 to 60 minutes, until the potatoes are tender. The larger
the chunks of potatoes, the longer is the cooking time.
Top with sour cream if desired, then sprinkle each serving
with fresh or dried lavender flowers.

Courage

Use these ingredients to boost courage, spark bravery, and to bolster resolve, tenacity, and confidence.

Allspice	Kale
Basil	Nutmeg
Bay	Onions
Black beans	Oranges
Black pepper	Oregano
Cayenne pepper	Paprika
Chili powder	Red beans
Cinnamon	Rosemary
Collard greens	Salt
Cumin	Spinach
Curry powder	Sunflower seeds
Garlic	Thyme
Ginger	White pepper

COURAGE SAUCE

Effects: Eat to increase courage and confidence, and to fortify resolve.

Makes: 4 to 6 servings

Ingredients

½ C mayonnaise

1 tbsp ketchup

1 tsp garlic powder

1 tsp chili powder

1 tsp paprika

½ tsp black pepper

Directions

Stir the ingredients together while you imagine yourself as a huge bear, lion, or other beast you think of as being fearless, brave, and fearsome. For a spicier sauce, add an additional ½ tsp to 1 tsp chili powder. Use the sauce on tacos, burritos, and wraps to add a kick of spice.

General notes

_____

_____

_____

_____

_____

_____

BLACK BEAN EMPANADAS

Effects: Eat to bolster your courage and confidence.
Makes: 4 servings

Ingredients

1¾ C (or 1 14.5-oz. can) black beans

¼ tsp salt

¼ tsp black pepper

¼ tsp cumin

¼ tsp chili powder

1 onion

1 clove garlic

2 C fresh spinach

1 tbsp butter

½–1 C shredded cheese (optional)

For the dough

3 C flour

½ tsp baking powder

1½ tsp salt

2 tbsp shortening

1 C warm water

1 egg

1 tbsp vinegar

Directions

Prepare the black beans and drain any excess liquid. Mix into the beans ¼ tsp salt, ¼ tsp black pepper, ¼ tsp cumin, and ¼ tsp chili powder, adding more or less according to your liking. Dice the onion, mince the garlic, and chop the spinach. Heat a tbsp butter on the stove over medium high heat, and sauté the onions and garlic until garlic is fragrant, and onions are translucent. Set aside and begin the dough.

Mix together the flour, baking powder, and 1½ tsp salt. Cut in the shortening, using a pastry blender or the back of a fork, pushing downward and dragging the tines of the fork through the mixture. Blend until crumbly, then add the warm water, egg, and vinegar. Mix it together to make a soft, sticky dough, adding more water one tablespoon at a time if necessary. Flour the outside of the dough mass so that it's easy to work with and no longer sticky. Let the dough rest for about 5 minutes on a floured surface. Divide the dough into fourths, then take each section and pat it out until it's about ¼ inch thick. Dust the top of the dough so that it doesn't feel sticky to the touch.

With a floured rolling pin, roll the dough out, fold it in half, and roll it out again to about ¹⁄₁₆ to ⅛ inch thick. It doesn't need to be exact, but if the dough is much more than ⅛ inch thick, it can be more challenging to get the empanadas to cook all the way through without burning the exterior. Cut the dough into circles using a wide-mouthed glass or cup. Put a few tablespoons of the beans and onion mixture into the center of each circle. Top with spinach, and add shredded cheese if desired. Wet your fingertips in water, and rub some water on the top half of each dough circle. Fold each empanada in half, pressing down the top and rolling the edge over to make a seam and seal it closed. Then use the back of a wet fork to press along the seam to further seal the edge. As you seal the empanadas, think of a positive affirmation with each one such as, "I am strong!" or "I am courageous!" Fill a deep pan with about ½ an inch of cooking oil, then heat on the stovetop over medium-high heat. Cook the empanadas in small batches, about 35–45 seconds each side until golden brown. Try with Courage Sauce to boost the flavor as well as the effect.

General notes

_____

_____

_____

_____

_____

_____

_____

_____

_____

_____

_____

_____

RED BEANS AND RICE

. . . .

Effects: Eat to encourage yourself to be bold, brave, and
   courageous.

Makes: 4 to 6 servings

Ingredients

2 C white rice (about 4
   C cooked)

2 15.5-oz. cans red
   beans (or 3½ C pre-
   pared dried beans)

1 green bell pepper

1 yellow onion

1 stalk celery

2 tbsp butter

1½ tsp cayenne pepper
   or chili powder

¼ tsp black pepper

1 tsp salt

1 tsp thyme

Sausage or vegetarian
   sausage (optional)

Directions

Rinse the rice, then put it in a pot with 4 C water. Bring
to a boil, then cover the pot and reduce the heat to low.
Cook for 15 to 20 minutes until all the water is absorbed.
Alternatively, you can cook the rice like pasta, boiling it
in a large quantity of water until the rice is tender, then
draining off the excess water.

You can use canned or dried beans for this recipe. If
using dried beans, be sure you prepare them in advance
according to package directions so that they're ready to
use by the time the rice is ready. Reserve the stock. If

using canned beans, reserve the liquid to end up with a soupier consistency, if desired. When the rice is nearing completion, dice the bell pepper, onion, and celery. Sauté these vegetables in the butter over medium-high heat for a few minutes until you notice a color change and the veggies become more fragrant. Once the rice is ready, transfer it to a larger pot if necessary and stir in the sautéed vegetables and the beans. If you're working from prepared dried beans, add about a cup of the stock. Heat at a low temperature for about two or three more minutes as you stir in the spices, adding more or less according to your taste. As you add the spices, envision yourself confidently taking action in bold and beneficial ways. Serve the rice and beans on its own, or top with cooked sausage or meatless vegetarian sausage-style patties or links.

General notes

Strength

Use these ingredients to enhance strength and stamina in times of emotional, spiritual, or physical weakness. These ingredients are also good for defense and protection.

Asparagus	Garlic
Beans	Kale
Beets	Nuts
Blackberries	Onions
Broccoli	Oranges
Chili powder	Peppers
Cumin	Potatoes
Curry powder	Radish
Eggs	Salt
	Spinach
	Turnips

STRENGTHENING
EGG NOODLES

Effects: Eat to increase your strength and boost your defenses.

Makes: 4 to 6 servings

Ingredients

¼ medium red onion

½ medium yellow onion

8 oz. egg noodles

2 tbsp vegetable oil (omit if using ground beef)

1 lb. ground beef or one 12-oz. package

meatless crumbles ground beef substitute

1 C sour cream

⅛ tsp black pepper

⅛ tsp salt

½ tsp garlic powder

Directions

Bring a large pot of salted water to a boil. As you wait for the water to boil, dice both types of onions. Once the water is boiling, add the noodles and cook until tender. As the noodles boil, cook the ground beef or vegetarian ground beef substitute over medium-high heat. (If using the meatless option, heat 2 tbsp of cooking oil in a pan on the stovetop on medium high heat. Add the meatless crumbles, and quickly stir to distribute the oil.) Add the garlic powder, and quickly stir the mixture again. Add the yellow onion and continue to cook the mixture until the onions are tender, stirring frequently. Think of the strength of the sun and the strength of the earth as the food cooks, and envision the power of the ingredients becoming stronger.

Drain the noodles, then stir in the sour cream, salt, and pepper. Top each serving of pasta with the meat or meat substitute mixture, and garnish with a sprinkle of finely diced red onions.

General notes

_____

_____

_____

_____

_____

_____

_____

_____

_____

_____

_____

POWERFUL PECAN
BRUSSELS SPROUTS
. . . .

Effects: Enjoy when you need a boost of extra power to overcome obstacles.

Makes: 2 to 3 servings

Ingredients

3 C brussels sprouts	½–¾ tsp salt
2 tbsp butter	½ C chopped pecans

Directions

Put the brussels sprouts in a pan, and add about ¼–½ C water. Cover the pan and heat over medium-high heat for about five minutes. Check after a few minutes to make sure there is still water in the pan; add more if needed. Once the brussels sprouts are tender (try cutting one in half to check), drain off remaining water. Melt the butter in a pan over medium heat, then add the brussels sprouts and salt. Stir to coat the brussels sprouts with the butter, then add the chopped pecans and stir again to incorporate. Cook for another one or two minutes, stirring frequently. When serving, top the brussels sprouts with plenty of the chopped pecans to give the dish a nice crunch and a nutty flavor. As you eat it, imagine yourself as a powerful giant and the brussels sprouts as full-sized cabbages. Think of each brussels sprout representing a problem you wish to overcome, and eat them as you envision each problem being easily solved.

FORTIFYING FRITTATA

Effects: Eat to boost inner strength and resolve.

Makes: 4 to 6 servings

Ingredients

4 medium potatoes
(about 1 lb.)

Oil for frying

1 small onion, diced

1–2 tbsp butter

6 eggs

1 can spinach (drained),
or 1 lb. fresh spinach
(chopped)

1 C shredded cheddar

¼ C sour cream

¼ tsp salt

¼ tsp pepper

½ tsp garlic powder

Vegetable oil

Directions

Cut the potatoes into quarters lengthwise, then cut each quarter into ¼-inch thick slices. There is no need to remove the peel. Fry the potatoes in about a half-inch of hot oil over medium-high heat, working in small batches. Cook each batch for about 8 to 10 minutes or until the potatoes are golden and tender. You can take a piece of potato out of the oil and test it with a fork: If the tines of the fork pierce the potato easily, they're ready. Preheat the oven to 350° F, and grease an oven-safe pan with butter or oil. As the oven heats, sauté the diced onion in the butter over medium high heat. In a large bowl, mix together the potatoes, onion, spinach, cheese, sour cream, salt, and pepper. Next, add the eggs, imagining yourself with superhuman strength and saying, "I can do it!" as you crack each egg. Break the egg yolks and stir the mixture only until everything is combined. Pour into the oven-safe pan, and bake for about 45 minutes until set and lightly browned.

General notes

_____

_____

_____

_____

_____

_____

_____

_____

_____

_____

_____

Section 6

✦ ◆ ⛥ ◆ ✦

Cooking with the Seasons

Find recipes and ingredients to celebrate the seasons and harness the power of Nature's tides.

Spring

Spring brings renewal, transformation, and inspiration. It's a good time to invite new beginnings and refresh your energies with ingredients that encapsulate the essence of spring. Spring foods include fresh herbs, green, leafy vegetables, plants with early harvests, and foods with a light, bright, fresh, or airy feel. Use these foods to bring new opportunities, invite growth, welcome positive changes, bring inspiration, renew, refresh, and purify, and to spark new love.

Artichokes

Asparagus

Avocados

Basil

Bean sprouts

Bok choy

Broccoli

Cabbage

Carrots

Cauliflower

Celery

Cilantro

Dairy products

Dill

Eggs

Fennel

Ginger

Green onions

Lavender

Leeks

Lemon

Lemongrass

Lettuce

Mint

Oregano

Parsley

Peas

Radishes

Rosemary

Sage

Snow peas

Thyme

General notes

_____

_____

_____

_____

_____

_____

_____

_____

_____

_____

_____

_____

_____

SIP OF SPRING SOUP

Effects: Enjoy to welcome and celebrate the blessings of spring.

Makes: 4 servings

Ingredients

2 carrots	2 green onions
20 stalks asparagus	½ tsp salt
2 C snow peas	½ tsp dill
2 C heavy cream	¼ tsp thyme
2 C water	2 lemons

Directions

Peel the carrots and slice them into thin half-circles. Trim the asparagus into half-inch pieces. Chop the green onions into ¼-inch pieces. Leave the snow peas whole. Heat the heavy cream, water, carrots, and salt in a soup pot over medium-low heat. Think of the earth warming up and the first plants of spring pushing up through the ground. Let the soup heat for about five minutes, then add the other vegetables, the dill, and the thyme, and cook until the mixture is steaming, the flavors are incorporated, and the vegetables are heated through. Do not let it come to a boil. Remove the soup from the heat, then zest the lemons. After the soup has cooled a little, add the juice and zest from one lemon to the soup, then use the lemon zest from the additional lemon to garnish each bowl. For a subtler lemon flavor, add the juice from only half the lemon.

VEGGIE SPRING ROLLS
• •

Effects: Eat to bring success and growth during the
spring season.

Makes: 4 servings

Ingredients

1 C green cabbage

1 C red cabbage

1 large carrot

1 C chopped bok choy

1 tbsp soy sauce

1 tsp powdered ginger

¼ tsp salt

1 tsp garlic powder

12 egg roll wrappers

Cooking oil

Directions

Shred the cabbage and carrots. Chop the bok choy into small, thin pieces. If you don't have red cabbage or bok choy, you can simply increase the amount of green cabbage to substitute for the missing ingredient. Mix the vegetables together in a large bowl along with the soy sauce, ginger, salt, and garlic powder. As you distribute the seasonings, envision achieving your springtime goals. On a plate, place an egg roll wrapper angled in a diamond shape, with a point facing away from you and the opposite point facing toward you. Place about ¼ C of the vegetable filling in the middle of the egg roll wrapper, then fold up the bottom point to cover the filling. Gently pull down on the filling to tighten it as you roll, much like a joint or cigarette. Fold in the sides, and continue to roll the egg roll upward and away from you. Use a little water on your fingertips to moisten the top point of the egg roll wrapper to help it stick and stay closed. Heat about ½ inch of cooking oil on medium-high heat in a frying pan on the stovetop. Fry the egg rolls a few at a time for about 1 to 2 minutes each side or until the exterior looks golden and bubbly. Use kitchen tongs to flip the egg rolls in the oil. Let the egg rolls cool for a few minutes before eating. Try with your favorite sweet and sour sauce, apricot sauce, or plum sauce.

General notes

_____

_____

_____

_____

_____

_____

_____

_____

_____

_____

PASTA WITH PURPLE CAULIFLOWER AND THYME PUREE

Effects: Eat to help usher in new opportunities for the spring season.

Makes: 4 servings

Ingredients

2 C purple cauliflower

1 C milk

½ tsp dill

½ tsp thyme

½ tsp salt, plus more for cooking water

8 oz. farfalle pasta

1 tbsp olive oil

2 green onions, finely chopped

Directions

Chop the purple cauliflower and boil it until tender. Drain it and put it in a blender or food processor. Add 1 C milk, then add the dill, thyme, and salt. Blend until you have a smooth puree, noticing how the ingredients transform when blended together. Think of anything in your own life that you wish to transform. Set the puree aside for now as you start the pasta. Bring a large pot of salted water to a boil, then add the pasta. Boil until noodles are al dente. When the pasta is a few minutes from completion, start heating the purple cauliflower puree over medium heat, stirring frequently until warm. Drain the noodles, toss with the olive oil, then top each serving with the puree. Garnish with a sprinkling of finely chopped green onions.

Spring Equinox/Ostara

Occurring on or around March 21 or 22, the Spring Equinox marks the official beginning of spring and the start of the time of the year when the days become longer than the nights. It's a time to celebrate life, hope, rebirth, and regeneration. It's also a great time to invite new opportunities and encourage growth, good luck, and success.

General notes

_____
_____
_____
_____
_____
_____
_____

EGG SALAD WITH SPRING GREENS

Effects: Eat to encourage growth and propel you toward your springtime dreams.

Makes: 3 to 4 servings

Ingredients

6 eggs

3 green onions

½ C mayonnaise

1 tbsp Dijon mustard

⅛–¼ tsp salt

⅔ tsp dill weed

Lettuce leaves

Directions

Place the eggs whole into a large pot. Make a wish on each egg as you place it in the pot, envisioning the success you desire and projecting the emotionally charged energy of your visualizations into each egg. Fill the pot with just enough cold water to completely cover the eggs. Bring to a boil on the stovetop over high heat. As soon as the water comes to a full boil, turn off the heat and cover the pot with a tight-fitting lid. Note the time, and remove the eggs from the water exactly 15 minutes later. Rinse the eggs with cold water. Once the eggs are cooled to a comfortable temperature, gently tap each end of the egg shell on a hard surface, then use the side of your thumb to gently roll the shell away from the egg. Keep your thumb parallel to the egg and rub the edge of the shell to loosen it from the egg.

Once the eggs are peeled, cut them into small chunks, about ½ inch or smaller in size. Cut the green onions into very small pieces. Place the egg pieces in a large bowl, then gently stir in the mayonnaise, Dijon mustard, salt, and dill weed. Add about half the green onions, saving the remaining green onions to use as garnish. Place a lettuce leaf on each person's plate, and top with a scoop of the egg salad and a sprinkling of the reserved green onions.

Beltane

Celebrated on or around May 1, about the time when thorn trees start to blossom, Beltane marks the unofficial arrival of summer and the fully fledged arrival of the growing season. Spring has truly sprung, and the earth is blooming once more. Beltane is a time to celebrate renewal, fertility, and creation, a time to glory in the beauty of the verdant and growing earth. It's a good occasion for inviting romance and letting loose, allowing love, enchantment, and joyful feelings to reign. Spells cast on Beltane for manifestation, growth, beauty, healing, purification, and love are especially potent. Spring foods as well as foods and cooking techniques attuned with the water element or fire element are very appropriate for Beltane.

ASPARAGUS WITH LEMON CREAM

Effects: Eat to celebrate spring and the earth's fertility, and to encourage feelings of passion, lust, fun, and frivolity.

Makes: 4 to 6 servings

Ingredients

1 lb. fresh asparagus

1 lemon

2 tbsp fresh basil

1 clove garlic

1 tbsp fresh rosemary

1 C heavy cream

¼ tsp salt for asparagus

⅛ tsp salt for sauce

1 tbsp butter for sauce

2 tbsp butter for asparagus

¼ C water

½ C shredded parmesan

Directions

Wash the asparagus and trim about an inch or two off the flat ends to remove the tougher, woodier part. Zest the lemon, then juice it, reserving both zest and juice. Chop the basil, mince the garlic, and take the rosemary leaves off their stems. Heat 1 tbsp butter in a pan over medium high heat until melted. Sauté the minced garlic, then reduce the heat to low. Add the heavy cream, then slowly add the parmesan, stirring gently and near constantly until melted and blended into the cream. Stir in the salt and turn off

the heat. Heat another pan over medium high heat, and once the pan is hot, add the asparagus and quickly pour in the ¼ C of water. Cover the pan and cook for 2 minutes. Remove the lid and let any remaining water evaporate, then add to the pan 1 tbsp butter. Add the salt and sauté the asparagus for about five minutes, then add the rosemary and basil. Sauté for an additional minute or two until the asparagus is vibrantly colored and tender. Think of the blossoming, fertile earth as the asparagus cooks. Add 1½ tbsp lemon juice to the sauce, stirring quickly to incorporate it. Think of your wishes for Beltane as you stir the sauce. For an extra lemony flavor, drizzle the remaining lemon juice over the asparagus before plating. Serve the asparagus with a thick line of the creamy lemon sauce down the middle, and garnish with lemon zest.

Summer

Summer brings a time of energy and excitement, growth and abundance. Success is in bloom, as the fruits of our labors begin to manifest. It's a great time for travel and adventure, friendship, love, and celebration. Try these summer foods to align your energies with the high vibrations and laid back yet passionate vibes of the summer season. These ingredients can energize, encourage happy feelings and spontaneity, improve luck, increase abundance, open doors for love, and invite success. Summer foods can be hot and spicy, or cool and refreshing. Some summer foods, like watermelon and fresh zucchini, can be very calming on a hot day.

Apples	Cilantro
Apricots	Coconut
Basil	Corn
Bay	Cucumbers
Beans	Lemons
Carrots	Limes

Marjoram

Mint

Mustard

Oranges

Oregano

Peaches

Peppers

Pineapple

Rosemary

Salt

Snap peas

Strawberries

Thyme

Tomatoes

Watermelon

Yellow squash

Zucchini

General notes

_____

_____

_____

_____

_____

_____

_____

_____

_____

_____

_____

TOMATO AND HERB SANDWICHES

Effects: Eat to invite love, happiness, and success to be yours this summer.

Makes: 2 servings

Ingredients

1 tomato

¼ tsp fresh thyme

¼ tsp fresh rosemary

4 slices of bread

2 tbsp mayonnaise

⅛ tsp salt

Directions

Slice the tomato into ¼-inch-thick slices. Finely chop the herbs, then mix them together with the mayonnaise. As you mix the mayonnaise, think of your desires for the summer and envision yourself achieving your goals. Toast the bread, then spread the herbed mayonnaise on two pieces of the bread. Arrange the tomato slices on the other two pieces of bread, and lightly sprinkle the tomatoes with the salt. Put the bread with the mayonnaise on it on top of the tomatoes to create two sandwiches.

ZUCCHINI PARMESAN

Effects: Eat to encourage the flow of summer's bounties to come your way.

Makes: 4 servings

Ingredients

4 zucchini

1 C flour

¼ tsp salt

1½ C panko
   breadcrumbs

¼ C milk

1 egg

Cooking oil

1½ C parmesan cheese

1½ C tomato-based
   pasta sauce

Directions

Cut the zucchini into ⅓-inch slices. Mix together the flour and salt. In another bowl, pour the panko breadcrumbs. In a third bowl, whisk together the milk and egg. After coating the zucchini with the flour and salt mixture, dip each piece first in the egg and milk mixture, then put it into the panko, coating both sides with a generous amount of the breadcrumbs. Heat about ¼ inch of cooking oil in a deep pan on the stovetop at medium-high heat. Fry the zucchini for about 1 to 2 minutes each side until the breadcrumbs are golden brown. Preheat the oven to 350° F, then pour a ½ C pasta sauce into the bottom of a baking pan. Spread the sauce around to cover the bottom in a thin layer. Arrange the zucchini over the sauce, then carefully drizzle the zucchini with the remaining cup of sauce, imagining a flow of good things into your life as you pour it. Use the back of a spoon to gently spread the sauce over any uncoated pieces. Add a layer of shredded parmesan to the top, and bake for about 15 minutes or until the cheese is melted.

General notes

_____

_____

_____

_____

_____

_____

_____

_____

_____

_____

_____

_____

_____

_____

_____

_____

PEACH MUFFINS
· ·

Effects: Eat to invite sweet blessings, love, and friendship
  this summer.

Makes: 6 to 8 servings

Ingredients

1½ C flour

1½ tsp baking powder

¾ tsp baking soda

½ C sugar

½ C brown sugar

½ stick of butter

1 can peaches (or 1¾ C
  diced fresh peaches)

1 C milk

1 egg

1 tsp vanilla extract

Directions

Preheat the oven to 350° F and grease a muffin tin. Mix
the flour, baking powder, baking soda, sugar, and brown
sugar. Melt the butter and cut the peaches into smaller
bite-sized chunks. If you're using canned peaches, you
can use your hands to easily break apart the peach slices
into smaller pieces. Next, mix into the dry ingredients
the milk, melted butter, egg, vanilla extract, and peaches.
Imagine the energies of the peach and vanilla resonating throughout the mixture. Spoon the batter
into the muffin tin, filling each one about ⅔
of the way, taking care to avoid overfilling the
cups. You'll probably have enough batter for

about 18 muffins, depending on the size of your muffin tin. Bake for about 20–25 minutes until they're a medium golden brown. Top with butter if desired.

Summer Solstice/ Midsummer

The summer solstice marks the official start of summer and the agricultural midpoint of summer. Though the days will still be longer than the nights, they will start shrinking in length little by little following the solstice as our earth reaches the point in its orbit where our hemisphere is angled away from the sun. Midsummer is a wonderful time for magick and enchantment of all kinds, and it is especially fortuitous for inviting love, passion, and excitement. Midsummer is a time to celebrate the good things in life and to revel in the blessings of the season. It's a night when the boundaries between the astral and physical realms are blurred, facilitating communication with Nature spirits and spirits of the dead.

PAN-SEARED PEPPERS WITH CITRUS SAUCE AND RICE

Effects: Eat to invite joy, excitement, magick, and passion on Midsummer Night.

Makes: 4 servings

Ingredients

1½ C rice

1 red bell pepper

1 green bell pepper

1 orange bell pepper

3 cloves garlic

2 tbsp olive oil

⅛ tsp salt

½ tsp oregano

For the sauce

1 C orange juice

1 tsp soy sauce

2 tsp sugar

¼ tsp salt

¼ tsp garlic powder

½ tsp toasted sesame oil

1 lemon, zested and juiced

1 tbsp plus 1 tsp cornstarch

1 tbsp water

Directions

Pour the rice into a pot and add 3 C water. Bring to a boil, then cover and reduce heat to medium-low for about 15 minutes or until all the water is absorbed and rice is tender. Meanwhile, cut the peppers into thin strips and mince the garlic. Heat the oil in a pan on medium high heat, and add the minced garlic. Add the peppers, ⅛ tsp salt, and the oregano, and cook on high heat stirring frequently until the peppers are seared and tender. Think of the magick of a moonlit night as you sear the peppers. As the peppers cook, warm the orange juice in a saucepan on the stove over medium low heat, and add the soy sauce, sugar, salt, garlic powder, and toasted sesame oil. Add the lemon juice and zest. In a small bowl, mix 1 tbsp water with 1 tbsp plus 1 tsp cornstarch. Mix until the cornstarch is dissolved, then pour the mixture into the sauce, stirring rapidly to incorporate it. Let the sauce simmer for a few minutes, stirring frequently until it thickens and the flavors come together. Fill your heart with joy as you mix the sauce and imagine the fun you hope to have. Serve the peppers over a bed of rice and top with the citrus sauce.

Lughnasadh

Celebrated on or near August 1, Lughnasadh marks the first harvest of the summer season. It's a time of showing gratitude for the first fruits of the harvest, celebrating the results of labor, and honoring the sacrifices that made it all possible. The earth and our efforts have nurtured the seeds we planted to full maturity. We are sustained and blessed by the earth, as well as by the efforts of both ourselves and others. Lughnasadh is a good time to acknowledge hard work and focus on feeling grateful. It's a good time for magick to bring increasing abundance, protection, success, and joy. Ideal for gatherings and games, Lughnasadh is a time to enjoy time with friends and family. You might celebrate with a picnic or cozy indoor feast featuring foods that showcase the essence of summer's bounty. Foods for Lughnasadh include bread, corn, and apples.

General notes

_____

_____

_____

_____

_____

_____

_____

_____

_____

_____

_____

HERB-INFUSED SANDWICH LOAF

Effects: Eat to celebrate the agricultural aspects of Lughnasadh and any other blessings in your life.

Makes: 6 to 8 servings

Ingredients

½ C oil

2 tbsp fresh rosemary leaves, chopped

2 tbsp basil

2 tbsp garlic powder

2 tsp yeast

2 tbsp sugar

½ C hot water for yeast

3 C all-purpose flour

1¼ tsp salt

½ C milk

¼ C plus 2 tbsp warm water

Directions

Heat the oil over low heat and add to it the rosemary, basil, and garlic. Once the herbs become fragrant, turn off the heat so the oil can cool down. In a small bowl or cup, mix together the yeast, sugar, and hot water. The water should be between 110 and 130° F. In a large mixing bowl, combine the flour and salt. Let the yeast water sit for a few minutes until it looks bubbly and has doubled in volume. Then add it to the flour and salt mixture. Next, add the milk and the oil containing the rosemary, basil, and garlic. Add more water a little at a time as needed to make a soft, workable dough. Dust the dough with flour and knead it on a floured surface for about ten minutes until it takes on a smooth and stretchy quality and no longer feels sticky. Think of the bounty and blessings that Nature provides as you knead the dough. Once the dough is kneaded, put it in a mixing bowl and let it rise for one to two hours. After the first rise, shape the dough into a loaf, and place it in an oiled bread pan. Cover the pan and let it sit for another hour to rise even further.

When the dough has risen, preheat the oven to 350° F. It's important to have the oven preheated before you start the baking process. Bake the bread for about 45 to 55 minutes until the top has formed a golden-brown crust.

Fall

Fall is a time of letting go and embracing change, preparing to head into the shorter days and cooler nights of the months ahead. It's a time to look within and take stock of your feelings, seeing if there is anything you wish to let go of or anything you wish to change as you head into the fall season. It's also a good time to fortify your defenses and bolster your strength and health as much as possible by eating good, healthy foods. Fall foods include root vegetables and other hearty foods that can be stored for long periods or preserved to eat through the colder months. Ingredients attuned with the Fall can be fortifying and strengthening, supportive and nurturing, inspiring and transformative. Use these foods to bolster health and vitality, to bring good fortune, to strengthen defenses, and welcome abundance.

Allspice
Apples
Beans
Black tea
Blackberries
Broccoli
Cardamom
Carrots
Cauliflower
Chocolate
Cinnamon
Cloves
Cocoa
Coffee
Corn
Cranberries
Garlic

Grains
Grapes
Green beans
Kale
Mushrooms
Nutmeg
Onions
Oranges
Oregano
Peanut butter
Peanut oil
Peanuts

Pecans

Pine nuts

Pomegranate

Potatoes

Pumpkin

Raspberries

Spinach

Squash

Star anise

Sweet potatoes

Turnips

Walnuts

General notes

_____

_____

_____

_____

_____

_____

_____

_____

_____

_____

_____

_____

_____

_____

_____

MUSHROOMS AND CHEESE SANDWICHES

· ·

Effects: Eat to embrace the change of seasons and honor the plunge into the darker half of the year.

Makes: 4 servings

Ingredients

8 oz. white button mushrooms

1 small onion

1 clove garlic

2 tbsp butter

⅛ tsp salt

4 sandwich rolls (bolillos or any other bread)

Cheese slices (any mild white cheese such as Swiss or provolone)

Mayonnaise

Directions

Cut the mushrooms into quarters and cut the onion into thin, half-circle slices. Mince the garlic. Melt the butter in a pan on the stove over medium-high heat, then sauté the mushrooms, onions, garlic, and salt. Think about the changes fall brings as the mushrooms and onions cook. Identify anything you like about the season and think about your wishes for the months ahead. Cut the bread rolls in half and place them in the oven on broil, cut side up. Once the bread begins to toast, remove it from the oven. Add cheese slices to the bottom halves of each bread roll and return to the oven for another minute or two until the cheese melts. Meanwhile, spread mayonnaise on the upper halves of the bread rolls. Once the cheese is melted, cover the cheese with several spoonfuls of the mushroom and onion mix. Top it off with the upper portion of the bread roll to create each sandwich. Makes four sandwiches.

General notes

GOLDEN SPICED CAULIFLOWER

Effects: Eat to give your personal power a boost as you welcome the transformations autumn will bring.

Makes: 4 to 6 servings

Ingredients

3 C cauliflower

3 tbsp butter

1 tsp garlic powder

1½ tsp turmeric

½ tsp chili powder

¼ tsp Chinese five-spice powder

¼ tsp paprika

¼ tsp salt

Directions

Cut the cauliflower into bite-sized pieces. Heat the butter in a pan on the stovetop over medium heat. Add the cauliflower and stir to distribute the butter. Sprinkle on the spices, noticing the uniqueness of each ingredient as you add it. Continue sautéing the cauliflower for about 7 to 10 minutes, until tender. Notice how the cauliflower changes in color, smell, and texture as it cooks.

DARK CHOCOLATE
AND PUMPKIN LOAF

Effects: Eat to invite autumn magick into your day.

Makes: 6 to 8 servings

Ingredients

½ C butter

1½ C flour

1 tsp baking powder

¾ tsp baking soda

1 C brown sugar

1 tsp cinnamon

¼ tsp nutmeg

1 15-oz. can pumpkin

½ C milk

1½ C coarsely chopped
    dark chocolate

2 tbsp cocoa powder

Directions

Preheat the oven to 350° F. Melt the butter. Mix together the flour, baking powder, and baking soda. Add the brown sugar and spices, then add the pumpkin and melted butter. Finally, stir in the chocolate and cocoa powder. Imagine your wishes for the day coming true as you stir in the chocolate. Bake in a greased bread pan for about 45 minutes, until baked throughout. Once an inserted toothpick comes out clean, the bread is ready.

Fall Equinox/Mabon

The autumnal equinox, also called the fall equinox and celebrated by many as Mabon, takes place on or around September 21 or 22. It marks a time in the year when the day and night are of nearly equal lengths. After this date, the nights will be longer than the days, and the nights will continue to grow longer until the time of the winter solstice. The fall equinox is a time to take stock of your life, establish balance where it is needed, and let go of things that are doing you a disservice. It's also a good time to give thanks for your blessings. The fall equinox is an occasion to celebrate togetherness and abundance, and enjoy the harvest's continued blessings.

General notes

_____

_____

_____

_____

_____

SQUASH AND CHEDDAR EGG CUPS

Effects: Eat to express gratitude and manifest more
blessings in your life as you celebrate the fall equinox.

Makes: 6 to 8 servings

Ingredients

3 C squash (butternut
  or yellow)

6 eggs

¼ tsp salt

¼ C milk

3 tbsp sour cream

1 C shredded cheddar
  cheese

2 tbsp flour

1½ C spinach

Directions

Preheat the oven to 350° F. Peel and cut the squash into
large chunks and boil the pieces until tender. Drain the
squash thoroughly, then mash it using the back of a fork
or the bottom of a sturdy, flat-bottomed cup. As you
mash the squash, think about the effort you put in and all
the work you do in your life, as well as the benefits your
efforts have brought. Add the eggs, salt, milk, sour cream,
and cheese, then stir in the flour. Grease a muffin tin, and
fill each cup about ⅔ to ¾ of the way full with the squash
and egg mixture. Bake for about 30 to 40 minutes or until
the egg cups are firm on the top and cooked throughout.
Hold your hand over the egg cups and give thanks for all

the blessings you have harvested at this current point in the year. As you enjoy the food, think of your wishes for the near future.

Samhain

Held on October 31, Samhain marks the final harvest and the end of the growing season. In ancient Celtic cultures and to many modern witches, Samhain signals the start of a new year as we enter into the darkest and coldest days of our annual cycle. Samhain is a special time to honor the cycle of death and rebirth as well as a time to pay respect to ancestors and remember all of those who have passed on. Communication with spirits comes more easily around Samhain, as wandering souls roam the earth in search of their loved ones or to seek revenge on this night. This night is a good opportunity for divination, prophetic dreams, spirit communication, and revelation, as magickal and psychic powers are enhanced at this time.

BLACKBERRY POMEGRANATE
SPIDER TRUFFLES

Effects: Eat to celebrate Samhain and to share as an offering for the dearly departed.

Makes: 4 to 6 servings

Ingredients

1 C blackberries

3 tbsp pomegranate juice

1 C chocolate chips

1 8-oz. package cream cheese

2 C chocolate cookie crumbs

½ C cocoa powder

Pretzel sticks

Directions

Let the cream cheese soften while you chop the blackberries and melt the chocolate chips. Put cookies into a sealable plastic bag and smash them to create crumbled pieces about ¼ inch or smaller in size. Combine the melted chocolate and pomegranate juice with the softened cream cheese, then stir in the chopped blackberries. Combine the mixture with the crumbled chocolate cookies. Put the mixture in the refrigerator for about an hour and a half so that it will be easier to work with. Pour the cocoa powder in a pile in the middle of a plate. Form the chocolate mixture into tablespoon-sized balls, then roll each one in the cocoa powder to coat it on all sides. Think of loved ones who have passed on as you coat the truffles. Place the truffle balls on a plate or cookie sheet, and chill them in the refrigerator for a few hours to help them set. Then stick four pretzel sticks into each side of each ball to create 8 spider legs. Break the pretzels in half to create shorter legs if desired. If you like, break off tiny pieces of the pretzel sticks to use as eyes for your spiders.

General notes

_____

_____

_____

_____

_____

_____

_____

_____

_____

_____

_____

_____

_____

_____

Winter

Winter is a season of looking inward, hunkering down, and tapping into energy reserves to make it through the harshest time of year. It's a time when sparks of joy and light tend to stand out and gain our attention, giving us hope to inspire us and love to nurture us. Winter is a good time for magick to bring hope, increase protection, and invite prosperity. It's a time of looking back at the months behind us and looking forward to the months ahead. Celebrate the season with gatherings of friends and family, sharing rich, sweet, or hearty dishes that showcase the luxury and pleasure of being alive.

Anise	Cranberries
Blackberries	Kale
Bok choy	Nutmeg
Cardamom	Nuts
Carrots	Onions
Chocolate	Potatoes
Clove	Snow peas
Cocoa	Star anise
Coffee	Winter squash

CARAMELIZED CARROT
AND ONION SOUP

Effects: Eat this soup to fortify your defenses and boost
your vitality and strength.

Makes: 4 to 6 servings

Ingredients

5 large or 7 small
carrots

2 onions

2 cloves garlic

¼ tsp salt for carrots
and onions, divided

4 tbsp butter

1 tsp salt, divided

½ C water for puree

3½ C water for soup
base

1 C milk

½ C shredded cheese

½ tsp oregano

Directions

Cut the carrots into thin rounds and the onion into thin
half-circles. Mince the garlic. Next, heat the butter in a
pan over medium-high heat. Add the carrots and garlic,
and sprinkle lightly with about ⅛ tsp salt. Let them cook
for about five minutes, then add the onions and sprinkle
with an additional ⅛ tsp of salt. Cook for an additional
five minutes or more, reducing the heat after the onions
have been cooking for a couple of minutes. Stir occasionally until the carrots begin to brown around the edges and
the onions are translucent. Next, scoop out about ¼ C of

the mixture into a blender or food processor with ½ C water. Blend until pureed, then pour the puree into a large pot. Add 3½ C water, 1 C milk, ½ C shredded cheese, and the caramelized onions, carrots, and garlic. Add ¾ tsp salt and ½ tsp oregano. Think of the energies of the ingredients melding together, amplifying the power of the soup. Imagine being full of energy, strength, and tenacity as you stir the soup. Stir a pentacle shape into the soup every so often to draw protective powers into the mixture. Cook over low heat for about ten minutes to allow the flavors to combine, stirring frequently.

General notes

_____

_____

_____

_____

_____

_____

_____

_____

_____

_____

_____

WINTER ROASTED
SWEET POTATOES

Effects: Eat to bring prosperity and encourage good luck.
Makes: 6 to 8 servings

Ingredients

4 medium sweet
    potatoes

3–4 tbsp olive oil

½ tsp salt

1 tsp nutmeg

2 tsp brown sugar

1 onion

1 tbsp butter

2 C bok choy

Directions

Preheat 350° F. Cut the sweet potatoes into 1-inch chunks, and place in a deep baking pan. Drizzle on a few table-spoons of olive oil, and toss the potatoes to coat them with the oil. Sprinkle on the salt, nutmeg and sugar. Roast for about 30 to 35 minutes or until potatoes are tender.

Cut the onion into thin slices. Heat the butter in a pan on the stovetop over medium high heat until melted, then add the onions. Stir frequently until the onions are soft and slightly translucent. Think of the positive aspects of the winter season as the onions cook.

Chop the bok choy into 2-inch pieces and add to the onions, envisioning the bok choy as money or other blessings pouring into the mixture. Cook for an additional minute or two until the bok choy is wilted. Lightly season the bok choy and onions with a pinch of salt if desired. Add the onions and bok choy to the sweet potatoes.

General notes

_____

_____

_____

_____

_____

_____

_____

_____

_____

_____

_____

_____

_____

_____

_____

_____

_____

_____

COCOA COFFEE WITH CARDAMOM-SPICED WHIPPED CREAM

Effects: Drink to warm up and revitalize your energies on a cold winter day.

Makes: 1 serving

Ingredients

½ C milk

1 tbsp sugar

1 tbsp cocoa powder

¼ tsp vanilla extract

½ C hot brewed coffee

¼–½ C whipped cream

⅛–¼ tsp cardamom

Directions

Heat the milk on medium heat in a heavy saucepan on the stovetop until it begins to steam. Add the sugar, cocoa powder, and vanilla, whisking rapidly. Take the milk off the heat to prevent it from boiling. Pour ½ C of your favorite hot brewed coffee into a large mug, then pour in the cocoa powder and milk mixture, leaving some room at the top of the cup. Add a few tablespoons of whipped cream, then sprinkle the whipped cream with an ⅛ tsp cardamom. Think of the cardamom radiating magickal power throughout the whipped cream and into the beverage itself. For a stronger cardamom flavor, stir an additional ⅛ tsp of the spice into the coffee and cocoa mixture before adding the whipped cream.

Winter Solstice/Yule

The winter solstice, happening on or near December 21 in the Northern Hemisphere, marks the time when the days begin to grow longer once more. As Earth reaches a point in its orbit where the Northern Hemisphere tilts toward the sun, we celebrate the return of the light and the hope of brighter, longer days ahead. It's a wonderful time to share gifts and show love and generosity. It's a time for optimism, hope, magick, and renewal.

General notes

_____

_____

_____

_____

_____

_____

_____

_____

_____

SPECIAL MEMORIES FUDGE

Effects: Eat to help create and retain good memories as you celebrate yuletide.

Makes: 4 to 6 servings

Ingredients

1 14-oz. can sweetened condensed milk

1 tsp cinnamon

2 C chocolate chips

1 tbsp butter plus extra for greasing

1¼ tsp orange extract

¼ tsp vanilla extract

1 C walnuts, chopped (optional)

Directions

Heat the sweetened condensed milk, cinnamon, and the chocolate chips over medium-low heat, stirring constantly with a wooden spoon until the chocolate melts and combines with the milk. Remove from heat, and add 1 tbsp. butter. Once the butter has melted, mix in the orange extract, vanilla, and walnuts (if using). Stir until the mixture looks smooth and no longer looks glossy. Think of the special moments that you would like to enjoy, and imagine looking back on this time fondly from a time in the future as you stir the fudge. Spread the fudge in a buttered pan, smoothing the top with a rubber spatula or the back of a spoon. Let the fudge cool to room temperature, then refrigerate until firm.

Imbolc

Imbolc marks the first signs of spring's imminent return. The ground begins to thaw in some places, and temperatures start to warm as the days continue to gain minutes and the nights get ever shorter. Imbolc is a time to look ahead at dreams for the near future, taking stock of what you have left behind following the winter, and making plans for what you would like to achieve come spring. Imbolc is traditionally a time to celebrate fertility and strengthen protections on your home, animals, and loved ones. It's a good time for magick to bring abundance, luck, and new opportunities.

General notes

CRANBERRY BREAD PUDDING

· ·

Effects: Eat to celebrate the good fortune that kept you through the winter, and to look forward with hope to the blessings of the coming spring.

Makes: 6 to 8 servings

Ingredients

8 slices bread

½ C butter

1½ C milk

2 eggs

2 tsp cinnamon, divided

½ tsp nutmeg

1⅓ C white sugar, divided

⅓ C brown sugar

2–3 C cranberries

½ C water

Directions

Preheat oven to 350° F. Break each slice of bread into 4 or 5 randomly shaped pieces, and place these pieces in a deep baking dish. Melt the butter and mix into it 1 tsp of the cinnamon and ½ tsp nutmeg. Drizzle the butter over the bread pieces. Then sprinkle on the additional teaspoon of cinnamon. Next, mix together the milk, eggs, ⅓ C of the white sugar, and the brown sugar. Pour this mixture over the bread. On the stovetop, heat 2 to 3 C cranberries, the remaining white sugar, and ½ C water in a heavy pot over medium-low heat. Reflect on the winter you're experiencing as the cranberries cook, and think about your hopes for the months ahead. Let the cranberries simmer for about 8 to 10 minutes until they are soft and sweetened. Pour the cranberry mixture over the bread pieces. Bake the bread pudding for about 45 to 55 minutes until the top is firm and bouncy.

Section 7

· ◆ ✩ ◆ ·

Ingredients

This section provides a reference enumerating the magickal properties of common ingredients while also highlighting some of the culinary uses and folklore surrounding these foods.

The superstitions and lore shared here are things I've encountered through my own experiences living in both the western and southern U.S., sharing recipes and culinary traditions with friends, family, and neighbors who share my passion for folklore and food.

Use the blank lines on each page to write in your own traditions, beliefs, notes, and discoveries about each ingredient so that this book is personalized to your own ideas and practices. Look here for inspiration to create your own magickal meals.

Allspice

Correspondences: Magickal power, luck, strength, protection, defense, passion, energy, courage, confidence, prosperity, health and healing, psychic vision

One of the "pumpkin pie" spices, allspice is warm, aromatic, sweet, savory, and robust, with a bit of a peppery bite to it. It's often described as tasting like a combination of cinnamon, clove, and nutmeg. Try it with roasted fruits and vegetables such as squashes, pears, and apples, or incorporate into meat rubs to add a complex layer of flavor. Heat some allspice in a pan on the stove or on an incense charcoal block to invite good luck.

Personal notes

_____

_____

_____

_____

_____

_____

_____

_____

_____

Anise

Correspondences: Magickal power, psychic power, luck, transformation, protection, purification, love, wisdom, communication, prosperity

With a spicy-sweet licorice flavor, anise is a powerful spice with distinctive flavor notes. Try in breads, soups, and stews, or add to baked fruit dishes. Use it on savory meats or roasted root vegetables such as carrots and parsnips to impart an exotic taste. Put some anise in your pillow to help ward off bad dreams.

Personal notes:

_____

_____

_____

_____

_____

_____

_____

_____

_____

_____

Apples

Correspondences: Love, joy, peace, friendship, health and healing, magickal power, psychic power, luck, friendship, wisdom, nurturing, beauty, abundance

Apples range in taste from sweet to tart. They can be eaten fresh or roasted in the oven to create a nice side dish or snack. Add fresh diced apple to tuna fish salad or coleslaw for a sweet crunch. Cut an apple in half horizontally and a star of seeds is revealed, a powerful symbol of magick. Recite the alphabet while twisting the stem; the letter it breaks on indicates the first initial of a future love.

Personal notes:

_____

_____

_____

_____

_____

_____

_____

_____

Apricots

Correspondences: Love, passion, joy, friendship, protection

Apricots can be eaten fresh or roasted. They have a sweet taste with a slight tartness. Try apricots in salads and stir fry dishes for a touch of sweetness. Use as a base flavoring for sweet sauces to serve over vegetables or meats. The kernels found inside the apricot pit are considered inedible; they can be poisonous. However, the pits aren't useless; you can bury them around your property line to help protect your place or carry on your person to help repel unwanted suitors.

Personal notes:

_____

_____

_____

_____

_____

_____

_____

_____

_____

_____

Avocados

Correspondences: Calming, dreams, friendship, ancestors, cooperation, love, beauty, fertility, abundance, passion

Creamy and refreshing, avocados are generally eaten fresh, when the outer skin is dark green and the inner flesh is tender but not super mushy. Avocados can be mashed and sprinkled with salt and lime juice to create guacamole, or sliced into spears or cubes to enjoy with toast, sandwiches, burgers, salads, tacos, burritos, and wraps. The avocado has been touted as a powerful aphrodisiac and symbol of love.

Personal notes:

_____

_____

_____

_____

_____

_____

_____

_____

_____

_____

_____

Bananas

Correspondences: Contentment, happiness, intelligence, love, calming, patience, flight, lunar energies, prosperity, virility

With their lightly sweet flavor and soft texture, bananas make a perfect addition to smoothies, milkshakes, and sundaes. Mix banana slices into a cup of yogurt, or tuck inside a peanut butter sandwich. Mashed banana brings sweetness, moisture, and body to muffins and breads made without eggs or sugar.

Giving or sharing bananas on a Thursday is said to bring good luck.

Personal notes:

_____

_____

_____

_____

_____

_____

_____

Basil

Correspondences: Love, luck, passion, prosperity, protection, strength, courage, magickal power, communication, cooperation, friendship

With a savory yet sweet herbal flavor, basil makes a great addition to sauces, vegetables, meats, and fruit dishes. Don't cut basil with a knife, as it will bruise and oxidize; instead, gently tear the leaves with your hands. Try adding basil to scrambled eggs for a savory effect, or use in tomato-based pasta sauces to bring out notes of sweetness.

Throughout the ages, basil has been praised for its magickal power as well as its flavor. According to folklore, if you silently hold out a piece of basil to someone and they take it from you, it's believed to be a sign of love and affection. Share basil with loved ones to promote feelings of friendship, love, and caring.

Personal notes:

_____

_____

_____

_____

_____

_____

Bay

Correspondences: Protection, strength, courage, health and healing, vitality, energy, psychic power, concealment, banishing, purification, success, magickal power

Earthy, floral, warm, heady, and aromatic, bay adds complexity to savory soups, meats, roasted vegetables, and sauces. Bay leaves are used whole, then removed from the food after the cooking is finished. The leaves are safe to eat but are hard and unpleasant to chew. Magickal lore holds that bay can aid in invisibility. If you want to keep a low profile and go unnoticed, try using bay to season your meals or tuck a leaf into your pocket or shoe.

Personal notes:

_____

_____

_____

_____

_____

_____

_____

_____

_____

Beans, Peas, and Legumes

(Green beans, red beans, black beans, peas, lentils,
black-eyed peas, chick peas, soy beans, tofu, etc.)

Correspondences: Protection, growth, strength, stability,
grounding, prosperity, abundance, health and healing,
luck, love, friendship, cooperation, success, courage

The many varieties of beans that have sustained humankind throughout the ages come in many colors and varieties. Most beans have a creamy texture on the inside, with differences in thickness of the outer layer and in subtle flavor notes. Brown beans tend to have a hearty, earthy flavor, while black beans are savory. Red beans are creamy and sweet, and white beans are often buttery or mealy. Dark red kidney beans have a tougher outer layer that adds a hearty bite to chilis and rice dishes. Green beans are the immature pods of the common bean plant. Peas have a fresh, mildly vegetal, slightly buttery taste and a creamy texture. Try beans in soups and chilis, and use beans to fill empanadas, tacos, and burritos. Eat green beans steamed or sautéed with a touch of butter. Try adding peas to fried rice and curries. Beans and peas have been used in fertility rites and agricultural rites, and given as offerings to the dead. Keep a jar of dried beans in the house to help attract abundance and prosperity. Black-eyed peas are considered to be especially lucky and protective. Off-white with a little black oval in the middle that looks like an eye, black-eyed peas are very reminiscent of the eye beads employed in many places around the world to ward off the evil eye and other misfortune. In the southern U.S., black-eyed peas are an essential part of the traditional meal eaten on New Year's Day to ensure good fortune in the year to come. Eaten alongside collard greens for prosperity and a chunk of meat or rice for good health, the black-eyed peas are believed to invite good luck and protect against major misfortunes. Peas have a lighter energy associated with love, peace, calm, cooperation, friendship, and joy. Use them to symbolize good luck and to bring peace and happiness to your meals.

Personal notes:

_____

_____

_____

_____

_____

_____

_____

_____

_____

Blackberries

Correspondences: Protection, defense, health and healing, energy, magickal power

Blackberries have a tart yet sweet flavor. If you're picking your own blackberries, choose the ones that are darkest in color and largest, as they are the sweetest and juiciest. Add blackberries to fruit smoothies or vanilla milkshakes to add extra flavor and a vibrant burst of purple. Blackberries are also wonderful in pies, cobblers, muffins, parfaits, jams, and syrups. Blackberry bushes are very prickly, and people have long associated the plants with defense and protection. They have also been used to encourage good health and fight off illness. Eat a handful of blackberries while walking the perimeter of your house or property line to help guard against intruders.

Personal notes:

_____

_____

_____

_____

_____

_____

Blueberries

Correspondences: Love, friendship, happiness, protection, health

Slightly sweet and slightly tart, blueberries offer a balanced and interesting flavor profile. Try them in muffins, breads, and smoothies, or toss a handful on a fresh salad. Add blueberries to your cornbread batter to give it a sweeter flavor. Simmer mashed blueberries in a small amount of water with some sugar to create a delicious blueberry syrup to use on pancakes and ice cream. These flavorful berries are associated with life, nourishment, and divine blessings. Blueberries can help ward off illness or shake off a blue mood. Share blueberries with the people you love to strengthen the bonds between you.

Personal notes:

_____

_____

_____

_____

_____

_____

_____

_____

Butter
(Plant- or dairy-based)

Correspondences: Ease, luck, escape, effort, reward, joy, abundance, prosperity

Even in small quantities, butter makes just about everything taste better. Add a small pat of butter when heating up canned or fresh vegetables to kick up the flavor and keep the food from sticking. You can also coat the inside of the upper rim of a pot of water or soup to prevent the liquid from boiling over. In many pastries, butter is essential in giving the food its texture. Homemade pie crust, for instance, gets its light and crispy texture from air pockets created by pea-sized chunks of cold butter surrounded in flour.

Whether you're using dairy butter, margarine, or your favorite plant-based butter, the key is moderation. If a recipe uses a lot of butter, keep portions small. Try infusing butter with herbs and spices such as garlic, rosemary, or cannabis, and keep on hand for a convenient way to add a boost of magick to toast and other foods.

It used to take a lot of time and physical labor to make butter, and people were very protective over the fruits of their efforts. Putting a piece of iron under the butter churn was believed to prevent anyone from stealing the butter. Like

any other slick, oily, or greasy food, butter can be used magickally to get things moving or to glide through troubles and escape from sticky situations.

Personal notes:

_____

_____

_____

_____

_____

_____

_____

_____

_____

_____

_____

_____

_____

_____

_____

_____

Caraway Seeds

Correspondences: Movement, transformation, mental clarity, psychic power, communication

Caraway seeds have a licorice-like flavor similar to anise and star anise, but it also has nutty notes that combine to give it an uplifting, exotic aroma. Try caraway seeds in rye bread and in other baked goods, or as part of a spice rub for hearty meats. It's also nice as a seasoning for roasted root vegetables such as carrots and parsnips. You can even try adding a pinch of caraway to your favorite tea to add complexity to the flavor and aid digestion. Caraway seeds can also be used to flavor stews and sauces. Just be aware that a little goes a long way! Start with a *very* small quantity, taste, and add more if needed. To bring psychic dreams, eat some caraway seeds or try some caraway tea before bed.

Personal notes:

_____

_____

_____

_____

_____

_____

Cardamom

Correspondences: Love, passion, balancing, charm, attraction, persuasion, protection

With a warm and spicy, slightly sweet, slightly citrusy, somewhat minty flavor, cardamom is a unique and highly prized spice. Use cardamom to season curries, beans, and rice dishes, or try it with roasted vegetables such as carrots, parsnips, potatoes, and cauliflower. Cardamom also goes well in spice cakes and breads. Hot beverages can also benefit from cardamom. Try it in tea or coffee, or add a light sprinkle to a cup of hot cider. Cardamom also makes an interesting tea on its own. Widely exalted as an aphrodisiac, cardamom is a useful ingredient in love spells. Chewing cardamom seeds is said to make a person more charming to others. Try chewing a few prior to any negotiation, interview, or sales pitch? Cardamom is also believed to have a protective power as well as the ability to balance one's energies.

Personal notes:

_____

_____

_____

_____

Celery

Correspondences: Calming, joy, peace, passion, growth, effort, health and healing, purification, strength

Watery and crunchy, celery can be enjoyed raw as a snack on its own or with some peanut butter, vegetable dip, or salad dressing. Try it in tuna salad, chicken salad, potato salad, and other cold salads where you want a little extra crunch. When cooked, celery takes on a slightly earthy and vegetal flavor. Add it to vegetable soups and rice dishes, or incorporate it in egg rolls and dumplings. In ancient Greece, celery was utilized in numerous ways. It was used as an aphrodisiac, and it was also left at gravesites to honor the dead. Wreaths of celery leaves were given to winning athletes at competitions. Try eating celery to boost your passion or to celebrate a success.

Personal notes:

_____

_____

_____

_____

_____

_____

_____

Cherries

Correspondences: Beauty, love, friendship, good luck, impermanence, fertility, health

Ranging in flavor from tart to sweet, cherries can be used in pies, cobblers, cakes, sauces, salads, and beverages. Add chopped cherries to whipped cream for a tasty treat, or heat with sugar and water to make a cherry syrup that can be used to top cakes and ice cream. Try adding fresh halved cherries to salads for extra flavor and texture. Carrying a cherry pit with you is said to attract love, while eating the fruit regularly is believed to enhance beauty. Drinking cherry juice regularly can bring good luck and boost protection against illness. Sharing cherries with a crush will bring to the surface any mutual attraction or hidden feelings. Eating a cherry with the pit still in it is said to be bad luck (plus it's a choking hazard), so remove the pits before eating the fruit. To give a person cherries is believed to bring them happiness and success.

Personal notes:

_____

_____

_____

_____

_____

Cilantro

Correspondences: Refreshment, renewal, cleansing, purification, movement, transformation, lightheartedness, cheerfulness, love, the spirit realms, spirit communication

With its lemony fresh taste, cilantro lightens and lifts the flavors of many dishes. Add chopped, fresh cilantro to tacos, burritos, salads, sandwiches, salsas, dips, and dressings. Use as a garnish for grilled fish or chicken, or add to sautéed mushrooms. Coriander and cilantro come from the same plant. In the U.S., "cilantro" refers to the leaves and "coriander" refers to the seeds. The seeds have a bright yet earthy, slightly nutty flavor with mild notes of citrus. In ancient Egypt, the seeds of the plant were considered to be enjoyable food for immortals in the afterlife. A bunch of cilantro hung in the home is said to bring protection. Cilantro and coriander have also been used in love spells. Try sharing cilantro with loved ones to encourage good times and positive feelings.

Personal notes:

_____

_____

_____

_____

Cinnamon

Correspondences: Magickal power, energy, passion, love, success, protection, prosperity, attraction, inspiration, enthusiasm, strength, confidence

Imparting a distinctive flavor and bite that is simultaneously earthy and fiery, comforting and stimulating, cinnamon adds depth and warmth to savory and sweet dishes alike. Use it to season roasted squash or pumpkin, baked fruit, chicken dishes, rice dishes, sausages, pies, cookies, cakes, and breads. Add to coffee, hot chocolate, or hot apple cider for an extra kick of flavor and an extra spark of magick. The smell of warm cinnamon will energize a household. Sprinkled on an open flame, cinnamon sparks. Utilize this effect by seasoning foods with cinnamon when grilling outdoors. Just be careful and take care that sparks don't land on hair, clothing, or any other flammables. Dishes containing cinnamon are great for a romantic meal. Eating cinnamon can encourage passion, boost energy, and increase excitement. Cinnamon is also believed to attract prosperity.

Personal notes:

_____

_____

_____

Citrus Fruits

(Oranges, lemons, tangerines, grapefruit)

Correspondences: Magickal power, success, health and healing, strength, courage, defense, protection, energy, vitality, joy, illumination, purification

From the sweet mandarin orange to the tart grapefruit and super sour lemon, citrus fruits come in a wide variety. For those who prefer their citrus fruits on the sweeter side, tangerines and oranges are good choices. Citrus fruits are great for bringing a light and lively, vibrant taste to foods. Try drizzling lemon juice on asparagus, green beans, fish, chicken, and avocado. Simmer orange or tangerine slices in water to create a base for sauces and syrups. Citrus fruits are believed to bring good luck while warding off and neutralizing negative energies. Lemons are used in many folk magick applications to absorb negativity and neutralize baneful energies. Eating an orange outside can improve one's luck and bring joy. Share citrus fruit with friends and family to show your love and express your wishes for their continued health and happiness.

Personal notes:

_____

_____

_____

Cocoa

Correspondences: Strength, magickal power, psychic
power, rejuvenation, courage, passion, love, energy, vitality, joy, prosperity, luck, protection, health and healing

Cocoa is the base ingredient of chocolate, one of the most
prized and beloved foods on earth. In Mesoamerica, cacao
trees were held in high esteem for the wonderful beans
they produced. These cacao beans were used to create the
world's first hot chocolate beverages, some of which were
alcoholic. Drinking it was believed to increase strength
and bring knowledge. Cacao was valued so highly that it
was used as a form of currency for many centuries. Drizzle melted milk chocolate on blueberries, strawberries,
cherries, bananas, and other fruits, or use dark chocolate
to add interesting undertones to savory and spicy enchilada sauces. Mix a little cocoa powder and some sugar in
your coffee to add an extra kick of energy and magick to
your morning brew. Give chocolate to those you love to
help ensure continued happiness between you.

Personal notes:

_____

_____

_____

_____

Coconut

Correspondences: Love, passion, fertility, beauty, dreams, psychic abilities, magickal power, protection, lunar energies

Coconut has a mild, sweet, and distinctive yet subtle flavor. Opening a coconut can seem daunting, and indeed, it's a task that carries some danger. You can buy shredded coconut, coconut flakes, or frozen coconut for a more convenient option.

If you opt for a fresh coconut, use an ice pick, Phillips head screwdriver, or sturdy metal barbeque skewer to poke a hole in one of the three darker colored indentations found on the end of the coconut. Usually, one of the spots is softer than the others. Drain the water from the coconut into a bowl and save to drink. Then wrap the coconut in a hand towel. Hold the coconut securely but keep your fingers out of the way as you give it a whack with a meat tenderizer right along the middle. Keep rotating the coconut and whacking it along the middle until it cracks open. Use a butter knife to carefully cut the meat of the coconut out of the thick brown husk.

You can simmer shredded coconut in a small amount of water to create a creamy coconut milk to use as a base for curries and soups, straining out the coconut pieces if desired. You can also use coconut in cookies, cakes, puddings, pastries, smoothies, and fruit salads. Coconuts are a lucky food for lovers, artists, poets, and anyone seeking inspiration. Coconuts are also good for amplifying psychic sensitivity. Try drinking some coconut water prior to doing divination or other psychic work.

Personal notes:

_____

_____

_____

_____

_____

_____

_____

_____

_____

_____

Cole Crops aka Brassicas
(Broccoli, cauliflower, kale, collard greens, brussels sprouts, cabbage)

Correspondences: Protection, strength, health, abundance, prosperity, banishing

The cole crops are actually all the same species of plant, *Brassica oleracea*, a variety of wild mustard. The plant has been selectively bred throughout the ages to produce a varied assortment of vegetables with very distinct appearances and flavors. While broccoli is green and cauliflower is white, yellow, or purple, both have crunchy stalks and flowering crowns that give the vegetables the look of tiny trees. Broccoli and cauliflower can be eaten raw or boiled, steamed, sautéed, or roasted. Their mild and vegetal natures absorb other flavors very well, so they work great in soups, pasta sauces, and casseroles. Try broccoli and cauliflower stir fried with garlic and soy sauce to give it a savory flavor. Spice broccoli with ginger or lemon to bring out its brighter notes, and season cauliflower with turmeric and garlic to give it a savory taste. Collard greens and kale both look like monster lettuces with big green leaves. Boil collard greens with salt and some vegetable broth or a piece of meat, or sauté in oil with garlic. Kale is great in a stir fry, or try brushing with oil and baking to create crispy kale chips. Mix shredded raw cabbage with mayonnaise, shredded carrots, and a little black pepper, salt, and sugar to create a simple slaw to top burgers. Brussels sprouts can be steamed, roasted, boiled, or sautéed in butter. Because of their appearance like tiny cabbages which make it easy to pretend to be a giant when eating them, brussels sprouts are excellent for magick to enhance your greatness and overcome obstacles easily.

There are a lot of spiritual beliefs and superstitions regarding cole crops. The ancient Romans associated broccoli with Jupiter and believed it to have protective qualities and healing powers. In the southern US, eating collard greens or mustard greens (a closely related member of the Brassicaceae family) on New Year's Day will guarantee prosperity in the year ahead, with the portion size in direct proportion to the riches gained.

Personal notes:

_____

_____

_____

_____

_____

_____

_____

_____

_____

Corn

Correspondences: Strength, success, protection, prosperity, health and healing, cooperation, friendship, joy

With its sweet and mild flavor, corn tastes good grilled, boiled, or roasted. Try sautéing a can of corn with a little butter and salt, or add it to soups, stews, and burritos. If you're cooking fresh corn, you can save the husks to use for arts and crafts. Alternatively, you can leave the husks on and cook the corn directly on the grill or in the oven; just start by soaking the corn in water for thirty minutes and remove some of the silk. Corn is sacred to many cultures, as it is an important part of the human diet. Hanging dried ears of corn by your front door is believed to draw in good luck. To burn corn, however, is considered very unlucky. According to superstition, burning the kernels can cause a person to lose money, while burning the cobs or husks is believed to lead to drought. Eat some corn or cornbread to attract wealth and health.

Personal notes:

_____

_____

_____

_____

_____

Cranberries

Correspondences: Cleansing, hope, purification, pres-
ervation, health and healing, peace, thankfulness,
prosperity, goodwill

Cranberries grow on sprawling, low-lying, almost viny
shrubs that prefer moist, marshy soil and bogs. Cranberries have a hollow, air-filled center that makes them
bouncy and able to float. They have a very tart, somewhat
bitter flavor that can be greatly mellowed with sweeteners
or added fruits. Try cranberries in muffins and breads, or
use as a garnish or sauce flavoring to add a touch of tartness to balance a rich, savory dish. Cranberries can also
be used in beverages like lemonades and teas, or frozen
to use as fun, colorful ice cubes to cool a drink or dress
up a punch bowl. One early American recipe for a tasty
relish called for cranberries to be ground together with
oranges, apples, and lemon. Cranberries are a symbol of
abundance, prosperity, survival, and the gifts of Nature.

Personal notes:

_____

_____

_____

_____

Cucumbers

Correspondences: Calming, cooling, relaxation, growth, fertility, healing, cleansing

Eaten raw, the cool, crisp flesh of a cucumber is very refreshing. Try cucumber slices as a snack, or eat on toasted bread with a little ranch dressing or mayonnaise. Mix cucumbers into salads and salsas for a refreshing crunch. Eating cucumbers will help relieve stress and cool tempers. Cucumbers are also associated with fertility. Consuming cucumber seeds is believed to help a person be more fertile in mind as well as body.

Personal notes:

_____

_____

_____

_____

_____

_____

_____

_____

_____

_____

Cumin

Correspondences: Strength, protection, defense, stability, grounding, health, courage, energy, stamina, tenacity, binding

With a warm and earthy, robust flavor that has a mild bite and a light hint of citrus, cumin brings an intensity of flavor best used in moderation. Try cumin in tofu and meats and in spicy sauces and chilis. Cumin originated in the regions surrounding the Mediterranean Sea. The spice was used to stop thieves, encourage fidelity, and keep pets and livestock from straying from home. To keep a lover or an animal from wandering too far from home, one only had to feed them cumin. To prevent theft, cumin was sprinkled in with the valuables, so that if a thief tried to grab the item, they would become stuck in the house and unable to flee before being caught in the act.

Personal notes:

_____

_____

_____

_____

_____

_____

Dill

Correspondences: Transformation, movement, communication, intelligence, inspiration, joy, calm, friendship, happy travels

With a vegetal, airy flavor and light notes reminiscent of citrus, dill weed adds freshness to creamy dips, dressings, and cold salads. Try it in egg salad or potato salad, or mix it on a mayonnaise and tomato sandwich to evoke the refreshing feel of spring. While "dill weed" refers to the thin, feathery leaves of the plant, dill seeds are also edible. Use the seeds of the dill plant as a flavoring when making pickles, or try a pinch of dill seeds in your vegetable broth. Putting a dill plant near the threshold of the house is believed to keep out any enemies. Eat dill when you wish to relax and have clarity of mind, or serve it to help lighten the mood, ease tensions, and soothe spirits.

Personal notes:

_____

_____

_____

_____

_____

_____

Eggplant

Correspondences: Psychic power, magickal power, defense

A member of the nightshade family, eggplants are technically berries that are related to potatoes and tomatoes. Their dark purple skin makes eggplant one of the most beautiful and unusual looking foods in the produce aisle. If cooked incorrectly, eggplant can be extremely bitter and unpleasant. When it's prepared correctly, however, eggplant's pleasant, squash-like texture absorbs whatever flavors you impart to it. To prevent the bitter flavor and ensure a great taste, slice the eggplant, rinse it very well, pat it dry, then sprinkle the exposed inner flesh with a little salt. Let it sit for several minutes before you cook it. Try roasting eggplant in the oven, or serve it battered or breaded and fried. Eggplant was once believed to cause insanity, and even had the nickname of the "mad apple." Eat eggplant before magick or divination to help sharpen your psychic sensitivity.

Personal notes:

_____

_____

_____

_____

Eggs and
Egg Substitutes

Correspondences: Fertility, binding, health, protection

Look for eggs marked free range or pasture raised that are certified humane, or buy local from a trusted farmer. Vegan egg substitutes can be used in many recipes calling for eggs. Eggs can be eaten scrambled, fried, or boiled. Aerated egg whites form the base of meringue and also help give souffles their fluffy texture.

To accidentally break an egg on the floor is believed to foretell important news. An egg with a double yolk is a sign of good luck or a possible marriage. If a double yolk egg is discovered during a pregnancy, it's believed to signal the birth of twins. When passed head to toe over a person, raw eggs can be used to draw out illness and negative energies. The egg is then cracked into a glass of water to be read for signs and symbols, then the egg is disposed of and the eggshell is smashed into tiny pieces and buried. As a protective measure, eggshells should always be broken into small pieces, as larger pieces can be used by one's enemies for baneful magick. On the

other hand, large pieces of intact eggshells are believed to attract fairies, which to many of us is decidedly desirable.

Personal notes:

_____

_____

_____

_____

_____

_____

_____

_____

_____

_____

_____

_____

_____

_____

_____

_____

_____

_____

_____

_____

Fennel

Correspondences: Health and healing, energy, protection, concealment, purification, safe travels, wisdom, transformation

Fennel has a very mild, fresh flavor with hints of licorice. It brings a touch of sweetness and adds complexity to savory dishes. You can use the feathery leaves as an edible garnish for soups and sauces and the bulb part much like you would use an onion. Try chopping the bulb into thin slices and sautéing it with other vegetables in a little oil or butter. Dried fennel seeds are also commonly used as a seasoning for both rich and light fare. Sprinkle a bit of dried fennel on cucumber salads, or try on roasts, in stews, in rich sauces, or on fish dishes. In Greek mythology, Prometheus gives the gift of fire to humans by hiding it amidst the large clusters of tiny yellow flowers that top the branches of the fennel plant. Fennel inserted in a keyhole is said to keep ghosts out of a house. You might try sprinkling some fennel seeds around the threshold instead to get the same effect without ruining your door locks. It's also useful to eat or have nearby when doing spellwork or taking other actions that you wish to keep secret.

Figs

Correspondences: Fertility, passion, love, beauty,
magickal power, abundance, prosperity, spirit communication, the astral realms

Figs are one of the earliest trees to be cultivated, with evi-
dence found of intentional fig tree plantings dating back
more than ten thousand years. Their fruit is rich, sweet,
and soft in texture with tiny seeds. Figs have an interesting flavor that's fruity with honey undertones. Try figs
with roasted pears, or add to cookies and granola bars.
Figs pair well with savory dishes, especially when flavored
with rosemary, basil, or oregano. Figs are associated with
fertility and sexuality, and they're also believed to help
facilitate spirit communication.

Personal notes:

Garlic

Correspondences: Strength, success, power, defense, protection, purification, courage, energy, health and healing

Fragrant and sweet with a savory bite, garlic goes well with a great many foods, from pizza to meats, sauces, stir fry, soups, stews, and roasted veggies. Try slow roasting garlic to bring out its sweetness. Mix roasted garlic with fresh basil leaves and olive oil to create a delicious pesto. Garlic loses its heat very quickly when cooked. Try adding tiny pieces of raw minced garlic to salsas so that it will keep its crunch and its kick. Garlic is associated with protection, and in folklore it's touted for its ability to ward off the evil eye and vampires alike. Eat garlic to boost defenses and increase strength, energy, and overall stamina and liveliness. Hang garlic in your kitchen to keep out danger.

Personal notes:

_____

_____

_____

_____

_____

Ginger

Correspondences: Magickal power, psychic ability, passion, love, energy, vitality, strength, healing, purification, transformation, excitement

Ginger adds brightness and bite to many main dishes, sauces, and sweets. Try ginger on tofu, fish, poultry, and vegetables, and add to Asian inspired sauces. Ginger is also good in sweet spiced cakes, muffins, and cookies. Eating ginger regularly is believed to increase energy, boost attractiveness, and make more opportunities for love, and sharing ginger-spiced foods with a romantic partner is said to bring good luck and passion to the relationship. Chewing ginger root or consuming powdered ginger is a useful charm employed by those embarking on an ocean voyage as a way to reduce motion sickness while at sea.

Personal notes:

_____

_____

_____

_____

_____

_____

_____

Grains

(Flour, flax, wheat, oats, rice, barley, millet, quinoa, cornmeal)

Correspondences: Health, longevity, prosperity, abundance, fertility, growth, stability, grounding

The many types of grains have kept humanity alive throughout thousands of years of difficult times. Able to be stored and very filling, grains continue to play a starring role in human survival. Grains can be ground to create flour which in turn can be used to create breads, cakes, cookies, pastries, and more. Try baking breads, muffins, and other baked goods with a combination of grains. Quinoa can be served on its own as a side or as an addition to soups, salads, and casseroles. Try mixing rice with different sauces to create new dishes, or add to soups. To ensure good luck, always break bread with your hands, as cutting bread with a knife is considered to be very bad luck. It's also unlucky to throw away stale bread—use it for croutons or bread pudding instead. If a loaf of bread has a very large pocket of open space inside from

an oversized air bubble, superstition holds that it can indicate a death of someone near.

Personal notes:

_____

_____

_____

_____

_____

_____

_____

_____

_____

_____

_____

_____

_____

_____

_____

_____

_____

_____

_____

Grapes

Correspondences: Good luck, prosperity, fertility, abundance, joy, love, inspiration, happiness, growth, health, vitality, virility, strength

There are many varieties of grapes, each with varying levels of sweetness and tartness. With their crisp and juicy texture, fresh raw grapes are an excellent and healthy snack. Try grapes in fruit salads, or mix grape halves into chicken salad for added sweetness and crunch. Grapes can also be cooked. Slice them in half and sauté or roast to serve with savory meat or vegetable dishes. Grapes are often enjoyed on New Year's Eve. Eating twelve grapes as the clock strikes midnight to ring in the new year is believed to usher in good luck and abundance in the next twelve months. The base ingredient for wine, grapes have long been revered and associated with good times and celebrations. The grapevine is a symbol of the Greek Dionysus and Bacchus, both gods embodying ecstatic revelry and passion.

Personal notes:

_____

_____

_____

_____

Horseradish

Correspondences: Strength, healing, banishing, defense, passion, energy, excitement, vitality

Horseradish has an intensely pungent, biting flavor that brings a lot of heat in small amounts. Remove the outer peel with a potato peeler or teaspoon. Then grate the root and mix it with a little vinegar right away to prevent the horseradish from oxidizing and changing its look and flavor. Grated horseradish can be used as a garnish or as a flavoring for sauces such as tartar sauce and cocktail sauce. Horseradish has been held in high esteem for its reputed aphrodisiac qualities and healing abilities. In modern American folklore, horseradish is acclaimed as a good ingredient to help chase off a cold or a headache, or to clear the sinuses. The horseradish has strong purifying and banishing qualities, and eating it can help shake off negative energies or end a bout of bad luck.

Personal notes:

_____

_____

_____

_____

_____

_____

Hot Spices and
Hot Sauce
(Black pepper, white pepper, cayenne,
chili powder, red pepper flakes, paprika)

Correspondences: Protection, defense, purification, passion, courage, energy, determination

Generally made from spicier varieties of peppers, hot seasonings and sauces are powerful ingredients that bring a lot of flavor and magick to many dishes. Hot sauces and hot spices come in innumerable formulations. They generally contain a mixture of hot spices and peppers that's very handy in a variety of recipes as well as in a variety of magickal operations. Add hot sauce to scrambled eggs, burritos, and rice, and sprinkle hot spices on fried potatoes and fried tofu. Hot spices and hot peppers are widely attributed with the ability to confer protection, banish baneful energies, encourage passion, inspire brave actions, and increase stamina and determination.

Hot, spicy foods have also long been used to curse and banish baneful energies. If there's a neighbor, coworker, or other person in your sphere you wish would move on somewhere else, prepare for them a special burrito. Be sure to check with the person beforehand regarding any allergies or food sensitivities, and be forthcoming about the ingredients when you serve it to them. Add some hot sauce with intention, thinking about the hotness of the spices driving them away when they eat it. Serve it to them and expect them to suddenly relocate within the next few weeks. *See also* Peppers.

Personal notes:

_____

_____

_____

_____

_____

_____

_____

_____

_____

_____

_____

_____

_____

_____

_____

Kiwi

Correspondences: Protection, success, surprises, happiness, optimism, love, health, hidden strength, wealth

While tough and furry on the outside, the kiwi fruit's inner flesh is soft, sweet, and succulent. It has a slight tartness that underlies a lively tropical flavor reminiscent of strawberries and bananas. Try eating plain raw kiwi slices for an easy and healthy snack, or add chunks of kiwi to a fruit salad or yogurt parfait. Drizzle sliced kiwi with agave nectar and sprinkle with chopped nuts or granola for a simple, healthy breakfast. Dreaming of kiwi fruit is said to be a sign of success to come, and if the fruit is eaten in the dream, it's believed to signal an influx of wealth. Kiwis are associated with love and romance, and eating the fruit is reputed to enhance feelings of passion and ardor. Eating kiwi regularly will help promote good health and positivity.

Personal notes:

_____

_____

_____

_____

_____

Leafy Greens
(Arugula, spinach, bok choy, chard, lettuce)
Correspondences: Protection, passion, energy, strength, courage, mental clarity, prosperity, abundance, health, defense

The term "leafy greens" describes a broad category of vegetables cultivated for their often large and edible green leaves. Some leafy greens, like romaine lettuce, are enjoyed raw in salads and on sandwiches, while others, like spinach and arugula, can be eaten raw or cooked. Try adding spinach to scrambled eggs, casseroles, burritos, wraps, and pasta dishes. Arugula leaves can be eaten fresh or cooked and have a vibrant, peppery flavor good in salads or with roasted meats or vegetables. Try sautéing spinach and arugula in a small amount of butter with garlic to enhance the taste. Leafy greens make for a simple side dish, a tasty garnish, or a healthful addition to stir fries, pastas, and other main dishes. Leafy greens are often associated with abundant wealth and good health. Eating leafy greens is believed to attract prosperity and boost vitality. In ancient Rome, arugula had such a reputation for being an aphrodisiac that the Catholic church forbade their monks from growing it. Eat leafy greens to enliven passions, improve vitality, attract prosperity, and boost energy. *See also* cole crops.

Personal notes:

_____

_____

_____

_____

_____

_____

_____

_____

_____

_____

_____

_____

_____

_____

_____

_____

_____

_____

_____

_____

_____

Lemongrass

Correspondences: Passion, psychic power, calm, joy, purification, communication, movement, transformation, happy travels

Citrusy and tangy, lemongrass imparts a fresh, lively flavor to stir fry dishes, fish, chicken, and sauces. You can buy it fresh, frozen, or dried. If using fresh lemongrass, you'll need to prepare it first: Trim off a couple of inches from the bottom root end, then cut off the green leaves, leaving about three to four inches of the bulb remaining. Remove the tough outer layers from the bulb, then pound the tender center in a mortar and pestle to release its flavors and aromas. You can dice the lemongrass to use in meat and vegetable dishes or leave it in one cohesive lump to flavor broths, sauces, and soups; just take the lemongrass out once the cooking is done as you would do with a bay leaf. Lemongrass can get things moving again if you're craving change when circumstances are stagnant. Eat lemongrass to refresh your energies, or to open the channels for the universe to send new opportunities your way.

Personal notes:

_____

_____

_____

Mango

Correspondences: Love, friendship, passion, flattery, beauty, dreams

Mangos have a very distinctive yet mild flavor that is primarily sweet with a slight tanginess and floral notes. Try using mango salsa to top fish dishes, or use it to add sweetness and complexity to savory grilled squash tacos. Mangos can be roasted, caramelized with sugar, or eaten raw. They can also be added to smoothies or used to top yogurt or ice cream. Mango is reputed to be an aphrodisiac, and eating a mango under the full moon will enhance beauty and attractiveness, increasing the chances for love and romance. However, drinking milk right after eating mango is considered unlucky, and doing so is believed to risk extreme misfortune.

Personal notes:

_____

_____

_____

_____

_____

_____

_____

Melons

(Cantaloupe, watermelon, honeydew)

Correspondences: Beauty, calming, happiness, health, abundance, good luck

Melons come in many varieties, with most having a sweet flavor and a juicy, crunchy, cooling texture. Most melons are eaten raw, but some can be cooked. Small chunks of cantaloupe can be roasted or sautéed to add to meat, vegetable, and rice dishes. Try freezing watermelon wedges for a cool summer treat.

Watermelons can be shared with family and friends as a way to celebrate and invite good luck and abundance. The deeper red the flesh of the watermelon is, the better fortune is to be expected.

Personal notes:

_____

_____

_____

_____

_____

_____

_____

Milk and Cheese

Correspondences: Fertility, protection, health, strength, calming, healing, binding

Milk and cheese are available in many dairy and non-dairy varieties, including vegan cheeses, oat milk, soy milk, hemp milk, rice milk, hazelnut milk, almond milk, and coconut milk. Plant-based milks and cheeses have varying flavors, so experiment to see which ones you like best. Milk is used as a base for many soups and sauces, and to add creaminess to dishes like mashed potatoes or certain risottos. Cheese is used to top many foods like tacos, burritos, and sandwiches, and it's also used in many sauces, casseroles, and risottos to give additional flavor and a creamy texture or act as a thickener or binder. Milk and cheese are symbolic of fertility, health, soothing, nourishing, and growth. For the highest quality milk with the most positive energy, obtain dairy products from the most ethical sources available, or use plant-based alternatives whenever possible.

Personal notes:

_____

_____

_____

_____

Mint

Correspondences: Refreshing, purifying, spirit communication, healing, energizing

Mint has an intensely cooling, refreshing flavor that brings an energy and lightness to many dishes and beverages. Mint is a wonderful flavoring for fudges and other confections. Just remember a little goes a long way when it comes to mint. Try fresh mint leaves in fruit salads and vegetable salads, or mix into couscous. Add mint to tzatziki sauce and other cold sauces where a cooling effect is desired. Put a sprig of mint in lemonade, water, and ice teas for a mild flavor, or add mint to brewed teas or hot chocolate for a more intense minty flavor. In Greek mythology, mint was associated with an underworld water nymph named Minthe, the daughter of a powerful river god. Legends describe how she was transformed into a mint plant by a jealous Persephone. Mint has long been touted for its abilities to heal the body, soothe the soul, and lift the spirits, and mint tea is believed to help people relax and open up to be more talkative.

Personal notes:

_____

_____

_____

Mushrooms

Correspondences: Connecting with spirits, psychic power, magickal power, transformation, peace, resurrection, revival, passion

Mushrooms come in many shapes, sizes, and varieties. Some are psychoactive, some are deadly, and some are absolutely delicious on pizzas, burgers, and more. Try white button mushrooms on sandwiches and pastas, or use portobello mushrooms for a more savory, almost meaty flavor. Mushrooms make an excellent flavoring for cream-based soups and sauces, and they are great in stir fry, on tacos, and in burritos and wraps. For a healthy snack, sauté some mushrooms and garlic and top with avocado or a light sprinkling of cheese. Just make sure the mushrooms you're eating are safe for consumption! Know what you're eating if you're foraging, and if you're new to foraging, have your mushrooms identified by someone more experienced. Mushrooms have long been associated with mystical qualities. Mushrooms grow in mysterious ways, often seeming to suddenly appear overnight. Wherever mushrooms grow in a circle, is believed to be a place where fairies have played. Try eating mushrooms whenever you wish to connect with the spirit realm and

be more sensitive to the entities and energies that roam the earth.

Personal notes:

_____

_____

_____

_____

_____

_____

_____

_____

_____

_____

_____

_____

_____

_____

_____

_____

_____

_____

_____

Mustard

Correspondences: Strength, magickal power, defense, protection, faith, tenacity, banishing, health and healing

Ground mustard has an intense, savory, somewhat biting flavor just like the popular condiment made from the mustard seed. Try mustard on roasted meats, or use in hollandaise sauce, barbecue sauce, and other sauces and dressings that can benefit from mustard's powerful flavor. It also gives a good balance and depth to dishes that feature a lot of cheese. A light sprinkle of mustard powder transforms ordinary macaroni and cheese into something more interesting and elevated. Mustard seeds are sometimes sewn into the seams and hems of wedding clothes to help ensure a strong marriage and happy partnership. A line of mustard seeds sprinkled around the perimeter of a property will help keep out enemies and intruders.

Personal notes:

_____

_____

_____

_____

_____

Nutmeg

Correspondences: Luck, magickal power, love, prosperity, protection, purification, courage, strength, psychic power, health and healing, prosperity

Earthy, warm, sweet, and aromatic with a spicy bite, nutmeg brings to mind fall weather and pumpkin pies. It makes a great spice for butternut squash or sweet potatoes, complementing the sweetness of the vegetables. It's also great in breads, cookies, and other pastries. Try using a hint of nutmeg in meat rubs and stews to add an interesting flavor note that helps bring excitement to a savory dish. Carrying a whole nutmeg in your pocket is believed to attract money and good luck. Nutmeg is also reputed to have the ability to support eye health if you're prone to getting styes. It's said that if you eat a teaspoon of raw nutmeg just once every year, you won't get a stye on your eye for the entirety of the year. Keep some whole nutmeg in your kitchen to draw in good luck, or eat before magickal workings to boost your power. Eat a peach sprinkled with nutmeg, cinnamon, and sugar to invite love and passion. Mace is another common spice, made by grinding the woody outer layer of the nutmeg.

Personal notes:

_____

_____

_____

_____

_____

_____

_____

_____

_____

_____

_____

_____

_____

_____

_____

_____

_____

_____

_____

_____

Nuts and Seeds

Correspondences: Strength, abundance, wealth, prosperity, growth, fertility, good luck, joy, love, calming, wisdom

From walnuts and sunflower seeds to cashews and almonds, nuts and seeds are rich and delicious. With a meaty, crunchy texture with varying levels of creaminess and earthy flavor, nuts are a versatile ingredient that can be used in both sweet and savory dishes. Try chopped nuts or sunflower seeds on salads, or mix into vegetable dishes like green beans or roasted squash to add body and complexity. Try slivered almonds on asparagus or fish dishes. Give almonds to those you love to promote peaceful relations and positive feelings, or eat to increase mental clarity. Almonds have a light, breezy energy useful in magick to bring peace, transformation, purification, movement, communication, and happy travels. Associated with luxury and good fortune, walnuts and pecans are both very hearty and rich in flavor. With their crescent shape, cashews have a connection with the moon. Eat them to boost psychic awareness and increase creativity. The chestnut is especially abundant with magickal abilities, believed to bring good luck and abundance when carried in the pocket, and being often used for divination rites. To see if a potential couple will be compatible, each person tosses a chestnut into a fire. If the chestnuts burn brightly and peacefully, it will be a good match. If the chestnuts pop, crack, and spark wildly, however, the pairing would be doomed to quarrels and misery.

American Chestnut trees once grew throughout the forests of the eastern U.S., reaching over a hundred feet in height and over ten feet in girth. The trees provided an ample supply of chestnuts for roasting and snacking that many people relied on throughout the winter. The surplus was sold in cities, making it easy to see why chestnuts are symbols of good luck and abundance.

Personal notes:

_____

_____

_____

_____

_____

_____

_____

_____

_____

_____

_____

_____

Olives

Correspondences: Peace, wisdom, blessings, love, longevity, tenacity, success, abundance, fertility, growth, passion, psychic abilities, joy

With a uniquely rich, delectable flavor, olives are a delicious and healthy addition to many foods. Try plain olives as a snack or appetizer, or add chopped olives to cold pasta salads. Use olives to stuff calzones, top pizzas, and enrich lasagnas. Try adding olives to macaroni and cheese or include on a cucumber sandwich for a fast and tasty lunch. A symbol of peace and divine favor, the olive tree has been revered and cultivated for thousands of years. In Greek lore, the goddess Athena is credited with giving the olive tree to the people of Greece. During the ancient Olympic games, crowns of olive leaves were given to the victors as a symbol of success and having the favor of the gods. Olives are also associated with love, lust, passion, and beauty, making them a wonderful aphrodisiac to share with a romantic partner.

Personal notes:

_____

_____

_____

_____

Onions

Correspondences: Strength, courage, purification, defense, protection, fertility

Ranging in sweetness and bite, onions are a flavorful and versatile addition to many dishes. Sautéing or roasting onions brings out the sweetness. Try them with other roasted or stir-fried vegetables. Try red onions raw on sandwiches, and use sweet Vidalia onions for onion rings.

Eat onions whenever you need to boost your strength, courage, or defenses.

Personal notes:

_____

_____

_____

_____

_____

_____

_____

_____

_____

_____

_____

_____

Oregano

Correspondences: Happiness, prosperity, good luck, strength, protection, magickal power, success

Oregano's earthy yet airy aroma and its savory sweet flavor make it one of the most well-balanced and versatile herbs you can utilize in your magick, in your cooking, and especially in your magickal cooking! Oregano is a key ingredient in many pasta and pizza sauces. It's also a good seasoning for potatoes, mushrooms, carrots, and peppers. Use it to flavor homemade broths and soups, and try it on fried tofu. Oregano is believed to bring happiness wherever it grows. With its ability to impart so much flavor, and its ease of cultivation and abundant growth, oregano is associated with happiness and success. In ancient Rome, oregano was worn at weddings to help ensure a joyful marriage. Oregano can be eaten to help attract prosperity or lift the mood. It can also be very protective and strengthening.

Personal notes:

_____

_____

_____

_____

Parsley

Correspondences: Protection, purification, defense, banishing, spirit communication, the spirit realm, health and healing

Although mostly known as a garnish, parsley is a highly useful culinary herb with intense flavor and lots of health benefits. Parsley has a very grassy, intensely vegetal flavor that works well as a flavoring for soups and broths. Try incorporating parsley into potato dishes, or use small amounts on pizzas and sandwiches. Sauté parsley in butter to use as a base for a flavorful sauce, or add to lasagnas or stuffed pasta shells.

Parsley has been associated with death since ancient times, placed on graves for decoration and used at wakes for its strong aroma. It was believed that saying a person's name while picking parsley from the ground will bring on the person a terrible curse. To protect a home from evil influences, parsley can be placed along the seams of doors and windows and any other openings or cracks. Placing parsley where your pets or livestock sleep will help keep them safe from harm.

Personal notes:

_____

_____

_____

_____

_____

_____

_____

_____

_____

_____

_____

_____

_____

_____

_____

_____

_____

_____

_____

_____

_____

Peaches

Correspondences: Beauty, love, passion, longevity, renewal, friendship, joy, peace

Sweet, juicy, and flavorful, peaches pair well with both sweet and savory foods. Try them raw or roasted, or use as a base for sweet and spicy sauces inspired by Asian cuisine. Peaches are associated with lunar energies. A gift of a peach invites peace. Eating peaches regularly will help preserve and enhance one's beauty and youthfulness. In the spring, peach blossoms often bloom before the leaves sprout, making the plant a symbol of life and longevity. To give peaches is a show of friendship and affection, and eating the fruit on special occasions will invite good luck.

Personal notes:

Pears

Correspondences: Calming, peace, clarity, purity, virtue, friendship, love, happiness

With a mellow sweetness and a cooling effect, pears bring delicacy and lightness to many dishes featuring rich nuts or savory pork. Simmer pear slices in a little water with some brown sugar to create a syrup to drizzle over crepes or pancakes. Pears can be roasted or enjoyed raw. Try adding pear to cobblers, crumbles, salads, and smoothies. It's bad luck to divide a pear between multiple people. A pear tree planted near the entrance to a home will invite good fortune.

Personal notes:

_____

_____

_____

_____

_____

_____

_____

_____

_____

Peppers

Correspondences: Protection, passion, strength, defense, banishing, cleansing, healing

There are hundreds of pepper varieties ranging from not at all hot, to melt-your-tongue spicy. The hotness of peppers is measured using the Scoville scale, where bell peppers clock in at zero, a jalapeño is in the 2500 to 8000 range, and the scorching hot Carolina Reaper registers up to 2,200,000. Prized for their intense flavors, illness-fighting antioxidants, and widespread reputation as an aphrodisiac, peppers truly pack both a culinary and a magickal punch. Peppers can be roasted, sautéed, or stir fried. Mild peppers like bell peppers and poblanos are great for stuffing with rice, beans, cheese, and other ingredients. Try sweet yet spicy banana peppers on sandwiches and pizzas, and add hotter peppers such as jalapeños and red chilies to burritos, tacos, spicy rice, and hot sauces. Burning peppers in the house is believed to chase away rodents as well as werewolves and vampires, while a dried pepper can be carried as a protective amulet. Red pepper powder can be sprinkled for cleansing and protection.

Dried red pepper is often included in magickal powders used to chase off enemies.

Personal notes:

_____

_____

_____

_____

_____

_____

_____

_____

_____

_____

_____

_____

_____

_____

_____

_____

_____

Plums

Correspondences: Good luck, love, abundance, dreams, relaxation, passion, beauty, protection, strength, longevity, health

Plums have a sweet inner flesh with a tart outer skin. They can be enjoyed fresh or added to breads, muffins, and puddings. You can also use plums as a base for sweet dipping sauces for egg rolls or fried tofu, or to add a touch of tangy sweetness to salsas used to top spicy veggie tacos. Plums can bring balance and complexity to many savory dishes such as roasted meats and poultry. For a sweet and simple plum dessert, try sautéing plum slices in butter along with a sprinkle of cinnamon and sugar. Serve with biscuits or top with a dollop of vanilla ice cream. Eating plums in the morning will guard against bad luck, and eating plums at night will bring deep sleep and interesting dreams.

Personal notes:

_____

_____

_____

_____

_____

Raspberries

Correspondences: Fertility, calming, healing, protection, friendship, happiness, purification, love

With a very tart flavor with slightly sweet floral overtones, raspberries have a lively acidity that goes well in juice blends and fruit smoothies. Raspberries are also great mixed into yogurt, oatmeal, or cereal. Try raspberries in muffins, or fill crepes with whipped cream and raspberries sprinkled with powdered sugar. Raspberries are believed to have a calming effect. Placing a branch from a raspberry bush near the front door of the home is believed to bring protection and good luck.

Personal notes:

Root Vegetables

(Potatoes, parsnips, carrots, turnips, radishes)

Correspondences: Root vegetables are varied and versatile. While potatoes are pretty neutral and nondescript in flavor, carrots are sweet and flavorful. Parsnips have a mild yet distinctive taste, with subtle flavor notes reminiscent of cloves or licorice.

Put a potato under the bed to ward off bad dreams. A piece of potato carried in the pocket is reputed to draw off aches and pains. Slice carrots into discs to resemble coins, roast in butter and brown sugar, and eat on New Year's Day to increase your chance of finding money and other treasure. Turnips were the original jack-o'-lanterns in Celtic lands where pumpkins were unknown. Try carving a turnip instead of a pumpkin next Samhain night. *See also* Garlic *and* Onions.

Personal notes:

_____

_____

_____

_____

_____

_____

Rosemary

Correspondences: Love, joy, peace, healing, communication, friendship, cooperation, courage, strength, purification, protection, success, magickal power

Aromatic, fresh, earthy, and a little piney, rosemary's lovely scent makes it a delight to cook with. Add to roasted meat or vegetable dishes. Rosemary is especially good with mushrooms, tomatoes, potatoes, and zucchini. Use it to season roasted chicken or turkey. Rosemary is believed to ward off evil and counteract harmful magick. Like oregano, rosemary is one of the powerhouse herbs that has just as many culinary uses as it does magickal uses. It can be used to attract love, encourage peace and cooperation, and inspire happiness. Placing a sprig of fresh rosemary near a grave is believed to bring peace to the dead and convey your love and respect for them. Eat rosemary to enhance your overall good fortune or to bring success in a particular endeavor. Think of what you would like to achieve when you add the rosemary to your recipe so that it will adapt to your purpose.

Personal notes:

_____

_____

_____

Sage

Correspondences: Fertility, health, healing, purification, cleansing, longevity, spirit communication, spirituality, wisdom, calming, easing sorrows, enhancing memory

With a vegetal and savory, earthy yet airy quality, sage brings a unique flavor profile and a delightfully aromatic addition to many dishes. Use sage in stuffings and to season roasted meats and vegetables. It's also a great seasoning for cream-based soups and sauces. An old superstition holds that eating sage in May will help preserve one's life. Growing sage in the garden is also believed to support a long life. It's said that success in business can be predicted by how one's sage is growing. Flourishing sage means a flourishing professional life, while withering sage reflects career trouble and a possible financial slump.

Personal notes:

_____

_____

_____

_____

_____

_____

_____

Salt

Correspondences: Purification, honesty, justice, wisdom, success, strength, energy, clarity, protection

A touch of salt enhances the flavor of vegetables, meats, and more. Even sweets like cookies usually benefit from a small pinch of salt. Use sea salt to add to your recipes the power of the oceans, or choose Himalayan pink salt to bring a more earthy energy with less sodium than ordinary table salt. Sprinkle on food to fortify the spirit, encourage honesty, or enhance wisdom. If you spill salt, toss a pinch of it over your left shoulder to avoid bad luck. Salt is also great for grounding your energies if you feel agitated or unsettled. Rub some salt between your palms to purify and refresh your energies. Eat salted foods to bring a comforting energy of stability. A little salt goes a long way; even if you only add a few scattered grains, its magickal qualities will still be imparted to the dish. If you think someone is lying to you, prepare them something to eat and add salt to it while saying, "Truth be told, or may the tongue ever thirst!" Guide the conversation toward the desired topic, then ask open-ended questions and listen carefully to the person's responses for admissions, confessions, and possible slip-ups.

Personal notes:

Sesame

Correspondences: Magickal power, protection, opening roads, strength, good luck, divine blessings, healing, beauty, longevity, inspiration

Sesame is used as a seasoning in the form of raw or toasted sesame seeds, or oil made from these seeds. With a nutty flavor, sesame adds depth and warmth to salads, tofu, sauces, and savory vegetable or meat dishes. Sesame seeds are also used in baked goods like cookies, hearty breads, and sandwich rolls. In Mesopotamia, sesame seeds and oil were considered sacred food of the gods. Offerings of sesame were given to the gods as a method of gaining divine rescue from misfortune. In Egypt, sesame was used as a beauty treatment, the oil being touted for its youth-preserving and beauty-enhancing properties. The phrase, "Open, sesame!" comes from the story "Ali Baba and the Forty Thieves" featured in *1001 Arabian Nights*. In the story, the phrase is used as magick words to open a cave of treasure. It's speculated that the phrase is inspired by the way the seed pod of the sesame plant bursts open up at maturity to release its seeds. *See also* Nuts and Seeds *for more seed foods symbolism.*

Personal notes:

_____

_____

_____

_____

_____

_____

_____

_____

_____

_____

_____

_____

_____

_____

_____

_____

_____

_____

_____

_____

_____

_____

_____

_____

Squashes and Gourds

(Yellow crookneck, zucchini, butternut squash,
acorn squash, spaghetti squash, pumpkin, etc.)

Correspondences: Grounding, calming, strength, peace,
calm, health and healing, growth, abundance, fertility,
protection, divine blessings

First cultivated in Mexico more than 8000 years ago and
spreading throughout Mesoamerica, squash has been
an important part of human civilization. Squashes have
a range of flavors that are generally mild and not over-
powering. Some have a buttery sweet, nutty flavor like
butternut, while others are more neutral and vegetal like
zucchini. Squash not only provides food, but also handy
utensils. Dried and cured squashes and gourds can be
carved into containers, cups, bowls, and spoons. There
are hundreds of varieties of squashes and gourds divided
into a few broad categories. Gourds are typically inedible
or at least not very tasty. Gourds are used for utilitarian
and decorative purposes once they have been dried and
cured. "Summer squash" is a term usually applied to thin-
skinned squash with tender, edible peels. Harvested in the
summer, and early fall, summer squash varieties include
zucchini and yellow crookneck squash. Try these squashes
steamed or battered and fried, or add to stir fry dishes.
Yellow squash is also great in casseroles. "Winter squash"
describes thicker-skinned squash that can be kept and

eaten throughout the colder months due to its protective peel. Winter squashes include spaghetti squash, acorn squash, and butternut squash. Try these squashes roasted and topped with toasted nuts, or use for soups and stews.

Squashes of all varieties have been revered in many cultures for their importance to human survival and culture. Most squash varieties have a comforting and stabilizing energy, though some bring a touch of something different. The butternut squash, for instance, is a hybrid created by a man named Charles Leggett who lived in Massachusetts in the mid-1940s. He wanted to create a large squash that was both tasty and big enough to feed a family. Leggett didn't consider himself to be a plant breeder, yet he followed his inspiration. Because of these interesting origins and its hybrid nature, butternut squash can be associated with inspiration, transformation, and revolutionary ideas.

Personal notes:

_____

_____

_____

_____

_____

_____

Starfruit

Correspondences: Good luck, prosperity, love, joy, generosity, magickal power

With a somewhat sour, somewhat sweet flavor, starfruit is delicious on its own or added to fresh salads. Slice a starfruit into cross sections to create little five-pointed stars, a symbol of magickal power and good luck. Try roasted starfruit slices as a garnish for baked fish or poultry dishes, or use raw starfruit to liven up salads made with dark leafy greens. With its distinctive shape, starfruit is considered a lucky fruit to eat to boost one's general good fortune. It's also believed to enhance magickal power and boost psychic abilities.

Personal notes:

_____

_____

_____

_____

_____

_____

_____

_____

Strawberry

Correspondences: Fertility, beauty, happiness, love, friendship, health, growth

A staple of summer snacking, strawberries are wonderful on their own or topped with whipped cream. Try fresh strawberries in water, smoothies, parfaits, muffins, pastries, dressings, sauces, and salads. Cut strawberries in half, sprinkle lightly with sugar, and roast in the oven for twenty minutes to create a sweet topping for ice cream and other desserts. With their bountiful growth and sweet flavor, strawberries are associated with fertility, love, and the goddess Venus. Sharing a strawberry with someone you like is said to encourage amicable feelings. An offering of strawberries given to the Fae or other Nature spirits is believed to attract good fortune. Give strawberries to friends to strengthen alliances. Carrying strawberry leaves is reputed to increase fertility and ease pain.

Personal notes:

_____

_____

_____

Tarragon

Correspondences: Protection, healing, passion, magickal power, purification

Tarragon has an intense flavor and a peppery bite, with notes of licorice and hints of sweetness. It's used to flavor light sauces, broths, vegetables, chicken, fish, and eggs. Tarragon pairs well with parsley, chives, basil, or dill. It's also great as a garnish. In Greek legend, tarragon is described as a gift from the lunar goddess Artemis. In more modern folklore, tarragon is associated with enduring passion, protection, and healing.

Personal notes:

_____

_____

_____

_____

_____

_____

_____

_____

_____

Thyme

Correspondences: Courage, bravery, strength, love, protection, spiritual power, joy, friendship

With a sweet and savory, earthy and floral, mellow and mild flavor and scent, thyme is the epitome of a well-balanced spice. As such, it goes with nearly any vegetable, meat, or egg dish, and also makes a great seasoning for broths, soups, and sauces. It's especially good on potatoes, tomatoes, and mushrooms. Thyme is a powerful herb believed to induce courage and bravery and enhance strength. Thyme has also been used to help ensure the dead a safe journey into the next chapter. Another use for thyme is based on the herb's association with Venus, goddess of love. Eating thyme or carrying it on your person can magnify one's attractive qualities and improve chances for love.

Personal notes:

_____

_____

_____

_____

_____

_____

Tomatoes

Correspondences: Love, happiness, passion, friendship, health, protection

Native to South America, tomatoes have been cultivated for centuries, prized for their flavor and versatility. Tomatoes can be slightly sweet or slightly acidic and are ideally well balanced and juicy, tender but not too mealy. Eat raw sliced tomatoes on toasted bread with mayonnaise and a light sprinkle of salt for a classic tomato sandwich, or use stewed tomatoes as a base for pasta sauces. Due to the tomato plant's relation and resemblance to deadly nightshade and mandrake, tomatoes once had a bad and mistaken reputation for being poisonous. Tomatoes have been both revered and feared for their reputed lust-inducing properties. In the Victorian era, tomatoes were considered a symbol of good luck. When moving into a new house, the family would put a tomato above the fireplace to bring good fortune and happiness to the home.

Personal notes:

_____

_____

_____

_____

Turmeric

Correspondences: Strength, defense, protection, courage, purification, banishing, joy, success, beauty, stability, good fortune

Turmeric has a complex, earthy flavor that pairs well with vegetables like kale, potatoes, or cauliflower. It also goes well with scrambled eggs, but using this spice in moderation is a must. Add turmeric to drained and mashed soft raw tofu along with some mayonnaise and a crunchy vegetable such as diced celery to create a tasty tofu salad. Turmeric is one of the base spices in curry dishes, giving the curry its yellow color. Turmeric is believed to have strong healing and purifying properties and it can be carried or eaten to boost protection.

Personal notes:

_____

_____

_____

_____

_____

_____

_____

_____

Vanilla

Correspondences: Love, psychic power, magickal power, luck, joy, friendship, cooperation, peace, calm, beauty, passion

Warm, sweet, and mellow, vanilla adds a great flavor to many baked goods, fruits, custards, and other foods. The vanilla plant grows in the equatorial region, and it takes several years for each new plant to begin producing seed pods. Within these seed pods are found the small, brown vanilla beans. These whole pods can be scored and used as a flavoring, or you can use vanilla bean powder created from the ground seeds. Extract made from the plant's oils can also be used to impart vanilla's flavors and magick to your foods. Try vanilla in coffee beverages, cookies and other sweets, on baked or stewed fruits, and as a meat rub for gamey or savory meats. Vanilla was prized in Mesoamerica, where it was used to create perfumes and incense and to flavor foods and beverages made with cacao. Carry a vanilla bean or eat vanilla flavored foods to invite love or luck, or to enhance psychic abilities and magickal power.

Personal notes:

_____

_____

_____

_____

_____

_____

_____

_____

_____

_____

_____

_____

_____

_____

_____

_____

_____

_____

_____

_____

Water Chestnuts

Correspondences: Calming, cooling, concealing, love, peace

Water chestnuts are an aquatic vegetable. They are not nuts at all, but rather corms, a specialized type of stem base that thrives in the marshy soft ground and muddy waters where the plants like to grow. Water chestnuts can be eaten raw, boiled, or stir fried. Pureed water chestnuts can also be used as a thickener for soups and sauces. Try chopped water chestnuts in egg rolls and stir fries. Since it grows in often murky water with the corms sometimes concealed in the mud, water chestnut is a good choice for magick to reveal, conceal, or cleanse.

Personal notes:

_____

_____

_____

_____

_____

_____

_____

_____

Personal notes:

_____

_____

_____

_____

_____

_____

_____

_____

_____

_____

_____

_____

_____

_____

_____

_____

_____

_____

_____

_____

_____

_____

Personal notes:

_____

_____

_____

_____

_____

_____

_____

_____

_____

_____

_____

_____

_____

_____

_____

_____

_____

_____

_____

_____

Conclusion

Incorporated throughout the simple recipes and ingredient suggestions in this book is plenty of room for customization. Don't be hesitant to try new ideas and techniques in the kitchen. A creative cook is a better cook, just as a creative witch is a better witch. As you use more magick in your food preparation, you'll find cooking takes on new layers of creativity and potential. The need for magick can inspire a meal, and the need for a meal can inspire magick.

Nourishing ourselves as best as we can with the best food we can acquire is important not just to our physicality but to our spirituality as well.

To disrespect one's body is to disrespect the divinity that dwells within us, whereas honoring our bodies with tasty, wholesome foods when possible reflects our gratitude and appreciation for the vessel that houses the sacred soul. Magick makes the process of cooking and eating more mindful and meaningful, calling our attention to the inherent power and characteristics of the foods we eat and bringing to the forefront our desire to thrive. Having dreams we wish to achieve and bodies that need to be fueled keeps us motivated to shape and create our realities. May the magickal recipes you've found in this book inspire you to transform your world through the power of food!

Bibliography

Agrippa von Nettesheim, Heinrich Cornelius. *Three Books of Occult Philosophy*. St. Paul, MN: Llewellyn, 1993.

Culpeper, Nicholas. *Culpeper's Complete Herbal & English Physician*. United States: Applewood Books, 2007. Originally published 1653 by Thomas Kelly (London).

Cunningham, Scott. *Cunningham's Book of Shadows: The Path of An American Traditionalist*. Woodbury, MN: Llewellyn Worldwide, 2011.

———. *Cunningham's Encyclopedia of Magical Herbs*. St. Paul, MN: Llewellyn Publications, 1985.

———. *Cunningham's Encyclopedia of Wicca in the Kitchen*. St. Paul, MN: Llewellyn Publications, 2002.

Digitalis, Raven. *Planetary Spells & Rituals: Practicing Dark & Light Magick Aligned with the Cosmic Bodies*. Woodbury, MN: Llewellyn Worldwide, 2010.

Kynes, Sandra. *Llewellyn's Complete Book of Correspondences: A Comprehensive & Cross-Referenced Resource for Pagans & Wiccans*. Woodbury, MN: Llewellyn Worldwide, 2013.

Marquis, Melanie. *Llewellyn's Little Book of Moon Spells*. Woodbury, MN: Llewellyn Publications, 2020.

Patterson, Rachel. *A Kitchen Witch's World of Magical Food*. Alresford, UK: John Hunt Publishing, 2015.

Porreca, David, and Dan Attrell. *Picatrix: A Medieval Treatise on Astral Magic*. University Park: Penn State University Press, 2020.

Recipe Index
by Ingredient

A

B

Banana

Happy Monkey Chocolate Banana Bread   103

Midnight Sundae   153

Smooth It Over Smoothie   130

Basil

Cheering Rosemary Basil Butter Bake   105

Herb-Infused Sandwich Loaf   191

Peace Pizza   126

Rosemary Tomato Bruschetta   122

Sweet Corn Casserole   118

Bean Sprouts

Cooling Cucumber Appetizer   36

Beans

Black Bean Empanadas   157

Checkerboard Beans   114

Easy Fire Chili   29

Harmonious Mini Chimichangas   131

Red Beans and Rice   160

Blackberries

Blackberry Barrier Cobbler   109

Blackberry Pomegranate Spider Truffles   202

Dark Chocolate-Dipped Blackberries with Mint   98

Black-Eyed Peas

Bok Choy

Broccoli

Brussels Sprouts

C

Cabbage

Cardamom

Carrots

Chocolate

Cilantro

Cinnamon

Cocoa

D

N

O

Plum

Pomegranate

Poppy

Potatoes

Pumpkin

R

Radish

Raisins

V

W

Water Chestnuts

Watermelon

Z

Zucchini

TO WRITE TO THE AUTHOR

If you wish to contact the author or would like more information about this book, please write to the author in care of Llewellyn Worldwide Ltd. and we will forward your request. Both the author and the publisher appreciate hearing from you and learning of your enjoyment of this book and how it has helped you. Llewellyn Worldwide Ltd. cannot guarantee that every letter written to the author can be answered, but all will be forwarded. Please write to:

Melanie Marquis
⁒ Llewellyn Worldwide
2143 Wooddale Drive
Woodbury, MN 55125-2989

Please enclose a self-addressed stamped envelope for reply, or $1.00 to cover costs. If outside the U.S.A., enclose an international postal reply coupon.

Many of Llewellyn's authors have websites with additional information and resources. For more information, please visit our website at http://www.llewellyn.com.